Music Therapy Training Programmes
in Europe: Theme and Variations

Edited by
Thomas Stegemann, Hans Ulrich Schmidt,
Elena Fitzthum and Tonius Timmermann

Musiktherapie Universität Augsburg

herausgegeben von

Hans Ulrich Schmidt und Tonius Timmermann

Reichert Verlag

Music Therapy Training Programmes in Europe: Theme and Variations

Edited by

Thomas Stegemann, Hans Ulrich Schmidt,

Elena Fitzthum and Tonius Timmermann

Reichert Verlag

Bibliografische Information der Deutschen Nationalbibliothek
Die Deutsche Bibliothek verzeichnet diese Publikation in der Deutschen Nationalbibliografie;
detaillierte bibliografische Daten sind im Internet über http://dnb.dnb.de abrufbar.

Gedruckt auf säurefreiem Papier
(alterungsbeständig – pH 7, neutral)

© zeitpunkt Musik. forum zeitpunkt 2016
Dr. Ludwig Reichert Verlag Wiesbaden
www.reichert-verlag.de
ISBN: 978-3-95490-179-1

Forewords

The first music therapy pioneers were self-taught. They introduced music therapy at a time when there were no music therapy training courses and therefore had to devise their own curriculum of studies and to learn by doing. Some of these autodidact music therapists were professional musicians, other doctors, health care workers, psychologists or teachers. As we can read in this book, there are now 119 music therapy training courses in Europe, many of these at a master level. This shows that the music therapy profession has undergone a major development. The pioneering period has professionalized music therapy services and led to the development of education and training. The didactics are based on the definition of music therapy professional competences and on the essentials in developing music therapy practice, theory, and research.

For a clinical profession like music therapy, it is important to formalize training. This is a move away from autodidacticism, although we should also keep in mind the importance of self-teaching and taking responsibility for our own learning. We still need to learn from our clients, from colleagues who perform music therapy in other ways than we do, as well as from colleagues from other professions. The book, "Music Therapy Training Programmes in Europe in 2016: Theme and Variations" demonstrates the progress towards formalized training and is thus an indispensable contribution to the profession. It gives a valuable overview, literally drawing a map of European music therapy training programmes and invites the reader to dive into selected programmes, learning about theoretical background, course contents, clinical training, and self-experience. The complexity of the music therapy intervention is made clear as well as the necessity for students to achieve advanced music therapeutic and academic skills, acquire knowledge about communicative musicality, music psychology, methodology, philosophy of science, and much more.

Edited by a team of experienced Austrian and German music therapy educators, this book represents a milestone for music therapy professional development. Comparing this development with a tree trunk, the 119 music therapy training courses illustrate the strong growth of the European music therapy tree; the trunk has grown solid, and the branches are reaching out and forming a fairly large tree crown. The branches, still not full-fledged, but steadily growing, may illustrate the expanding music therapy profession, whereas the roots may illustrate the music therapy discipline, soundly grounded in fertile soil, and enriched by a composite body of knowledge. This is what forms the training of music therapy students.

For the European music therapy community, this book is inspiring and enriching. It represents an important contribution to the didactics and confirms the growth of a young profession.

Prof. Dr. Hanne Mette Ridder
President of the European Music Therapy Confederation

The development of a training programme that teaches the experience-based and knowledge-based field of music therapy as an artistic-scientific subject, depends on various disciplines and institutions. The pioneers in Europe were musicians, instrument pedagogues, psychiatrists, musicologists, who, coming from different backgrounds, and working in music high schools and clinics, entered into a dialogue.

The trigger for this was often a personal key moment in the middle of life after a successful professional career, whereby the interest in music therapy arose (Juliette Alvin, Johannes T. Eschen, Clemens Holthaus, Editha Koffer-Ullrich, Gertrud K. Loos, Paul Nordoff, Gertrud Orff, Serafina Poch, Mary Priestley, Clive Robbins, Alfred Schmölz, Christoph Schwabe, et al.).

These music therapy pioneers developed their own specific way of working according to their area of work and interest, which, in the course of time, was transferred by their students on to new fields of treatment. Of course, an unbelievable variety and wide spectrum developed from this, which is now taught in training programmes.

In 1970, Karin Reissenberger (today K. Schumacher) was the first to record the scene through personal encounters, above all with H. Teirich (1958), journeys through the whole of Europe and a questionnaire sent by post. In 1996 at the world congress in Hamburg, Denise Grocke and Tony Wigram (World Federation of Music Therapy, WFMT) published the first international survey about world-wide training programmes.

According to these terms of reference, Monika Nöcker-Ribaupierre presented an overview of the 60 accredited European training programmes (BA and MA level) in 2005 at the conference of the EMTC (European Music Therapy Confederation) in Bologna, Italy. In 2014, with the help of the internet, Johanna Schmid published an overview of all 117 European training programmes, of which 66 are not (yet) accredited. This latest overview from the 27 EMTC member countries shows how the scene has grown (from 2005 – 2014: 11 vs. 18 BA, 30 vs. 45 MA) and where in Europe which kind of training programme has developed.

This variety has developed from individual initiatives, according to regional and personal possibilities. Apart from the curricula of these training programmes it is evident that even greater differences exist: on prerequisites, content orientation and above all the extent of the training. This makes the scene difficult to define on a political professional level. The leap to establish music therapy as an academic course of study throughout Europe has not yet been achieved, but we are on the way. Up till now, the profession is only recognized in five European countries, in Austria, Lithuania, Latvia in its own music therapy law, and in the UK and in Israel within arts therapies, and thereby protected.

Other countries have formulated their own quality standards for their own certification, which is paid for by some social or health systems (the Nordic countries, Belgium, Switzerland, the Netherlands), or are integrated in the health system (Germany). In many countries it is still possible to create training programmes that do not accord with the officially developed national standards.

Now a review of the position of the EMTC: According to the terms of reference of the Bologna Treaty of 1999 the academic courses of study are obliged to develop their training programmes according to higher education standards of Bachelor and Master level's qualification. This approach has been strongly recommended by the EMTC for all European countries. Going from these Bologna terms of reference, the EMTC has recently formulated standards of quality for European certified music therapists for BA, MA, and for supervision (see http://emtc-eu.com/register).

On the European level it is not possible for a profession to be recognized without generally valid formulation and adhering to such high standards of quality. The task of the EMTC delegates is to provide this connection and international network and herewith support their countries in developing our profession to the highest possible level. As one can see, these efforts are fruitful. However, the standards of quality for the content of BA/MA are not defined Europe-wide. The content of the academic degrees BA and MA lies in the responsibility of the countries, whose parameters are mostly determined by the EU, but they are ultimately the responsibility of the individual countries.

The EMTC also has no legislative powers to this effect – it is an organisation for quality assurance, that, based on wide international recognition, strengthens the profession of music therapy and ensures its development. The already existing training programmes should try to achieve such professional standards that many re-accredited training programmes already have as national guidelines. Only a harmonisation of qualitative educational standards will enable a wider recognition of music therapy.

Already in 1979, W. Strobel and G. Huppmann formulated the idea of a specialized music therapist. Their foresight seems to be confirmed today in clinical practice, where music therapists increasingly specialize in one field and organize themselves into specific national and international work groups. There are even already some training programmes (e.g. the programme in Würzburg, Germany focussing on dementia and clients with special needs) where this is reflected. Also, nowadays, a paradigm change is looming; here the focus is not only on qualified training programmes, but additionally on the question of which training can be best applied to which clinical condition.

Which physical-emotional problem, disorder, illness can be treated in the best way by which music therapy method? Which interdisciplinary specializations should work together in order to achieve a theoretical basis for a specific way of working, and thereby asking the correct research and evaluation questions? Fundamentally, self-reflective subjects should be offered in all training programmes, influencing and forming the personality of the students. Findings from surveys on graduates of training programmes show that this content is considered as especially important (see Ruess & Bauer, 2015). One of the most interesting questions remains that of how the medium of music is taught in general, and also especially for the different ways of working. How much ability on which instruments should be demanded as prerequisites for the often relatively short training programme and how should musicianship with regard to its therapeutic application be taught?

This book shows a selection of the various music therapeutic training programmes in different parts of Europe that are depicted according to academic development, research, recognition. The training programmes presented here represent different philosophies of training, different schools of music therapy and current information on academic and health organisations. We recommend that apart from most of the contents which are comparable, each training programme should teach the European and national history of music therapy in order to impart to the students the special base that our profession developed from – and to strengthen their feeling for the value of individual initiative and responsibility. In this way, the work of many music therapists who made the beginnings of music therapy in Europe possible and laid the foundation for the development, upsurge and recognition of it over the last 60 years can be valued. This can hopefully contribute to imparting to the students the fundamental strength of the international music therapy community and to stimulate their curiosity and engagement for the world of music therapy.

Dr. sc. mus. Monika Nöcker-Ribaupierre

Past Secretary General and Vice-President EMTC, founder of the Music Therapy Training BWM at Freies Musikzentrum München

Prof. Dr. rer. sc. mus. Karin Schumacher

Music therapist (DMtG), founder of the music therapy programme at the University of the Arts Berlin

References and further reading

De Backer, J., Nöcker-Ribaupierre & M., Sutton, J. (2014). The identity and professionalization of European music therapy, with an overview and history of the European Music Therapy Confederation. In J. De Backer & J. Sutton (Eds.), *The music in music therapy. Psychodynamic music therapy in Europe* (pp. 24-36). London: Jessica Kingsley.

Grocke, D. & Wigram, T. (1996). *World survey on music therapy training courses.* Paper presented at 8th World Congress of Music Therapy, Hamburg, Germany.

Nöcker-Ribaupierre, M. (2005). *Training courses in Europe.* Paper presented at music therapy conference in Bologna, Italy. www.emtc-eu.com

Nöcker-Ribaupierre, M. (2010/2014). *Beginning and theoretical orientations of music therapy in Europe.* Retrieved April 21, 2016 from www.emtc-eu.com

Nöcker-Ribaupierre, M. (2013). Research overview of German speaking countries. *Voices: A World Forum for Music Therapy, 13*(2). DOI: http://dx.doi.org/10.15845/voices.v13i2

Nöcker-Ribaupierre, M. (2015). The European Music Therapy Confederation – history and development. *Approaches: Music Therapy & Special Music Education, Special Issue 7*(1), 23-29.

Nöcker-Ribaupierre, M. (2016). Recognition of music therapy in Europe. In J. Edwards (Ed.), *The Oxford handbook of music therapy* (pp. 929-937). Oxford: Oxford University Press.

Reissenberger, K. (1973). Zum Stand der Musiktherapie in europäischen Ländern und den USA [On the status of music therapy in European countries and the USA]. In M. Geck (Ed.), *Musiktherapie als Problem der Gesellschaft* [Music therapy as a societal problem]. Stuttgart: Klett.

Reissenberger, K. (1970). *Versuch einer Überschau musiktherapeutischer Bemühungen innerhalb des europäischen Raumes* [Attempt of an overview of music therapeutic efforts within the European area]. Unpublished diploma thesis, Akademie für Musik und darstellende Kunst Wien, Vienna.

Ruess, J. & Bauer, S. (2015). *Questionnaire of the alumni survey for the music therapy training program at the University of the Arts Berlin.* Unpublished diploma thesis, University of the Arts, Berlin.

Schmid, J. (2014). *Music Therapy Training Courses in Europe.* Unpublished diploma thesis, Universität für Musik und darstellende Kunst Wien, Vienna.

Strobel, W. & Huppmann, G. (1979). *Musiktherapie. Grundlagen, Formen, Möglichkeiten* [Music therapy. Foundations, approaches, possibilities]. Göttingen: Hogrefe.

Teirich, H. (1958). *Musik in der Medizin* [Music in medicine]. Stuttgart: G. Fischer.

Contents

1 Introduction

Thomas Stegemann, Hans Ulrich Schmidt, Elena Fitzthum and Tonius Timmermann

Why write a book on music therapy training programmes in Europe?

The editors of the present book are music therapists – coming from various professional and musical backgrounds. Different paths led them to music therapy: Elena Fitzthum studied piano before she decided to move to Vienna to start something completely new. Tonius Timmermann was a music teacher for some time before he enrolled at the University of Music and Performing Arts Vienna, Austria at the end of the 1970s. Hans Ulrich Schmidt and Thomas Stegemann both studied music, music therapy and medicine, and specialised in psychosomatic medicine (HUS), respectively in child and adolescents psychiatry to later undertake further qualifications in family therapy (TS). Two of the editors are pianists (EF, HUS), one plays piano, guitar and monochord (TT), and one dedicated himself to the guitar (TS). Today, all of them are experienced university teachers, and are also involved in advocacy. In addition, they are heads of music therapy training courses (Vienna, Austria/Augsburg, Germany), and/or have been involved in the development of training programmes (Vienna, Austria/Augsburg, Germany/Munich, Germany).

Working in the field of education – designing, revising, or streamlining a curriculum – some questions come up repeatedly: How do they do it in other institutes or in other countries? How do others deal with a certain issue? Who is experienced with a distinct problem? Does one really have to reinvent the wheel?

To date, there is no publication that covers the above mentioned questions. Despite the manifold sources on the internet, there is no systematic overview of European music therapy training programmes. Hence, the four authors came up with the idea of collecting this data and to publish it in English to reach as many people as possible interested in this topic and struggling with the same questions. Once the project was underway, it seemed natural to target the 10th European Music Therapy Conference 2016 in Vienna, Austria as a release date – and here it is!

Our aim was not only to provide an overview of the current situation of music therapy training programmes in Europe, but to also give detailed insights into the structure and the content of music therapy training courses in different European countries. Of course, it was not possible to include all of the next to 120 current music therapy training programmes in Europe in this book. Instead we endeavoured to portray a selection of ten degree programmes from various countries, covering the three European regions according to EMTC's organisational structure: North, Middle and South of Europe. In addition, we strived to include different music therapy backgrounds, approaches, phases of institutional developments, different healthcare systems, different status of legal recognition of music therapy, and so on. Of course, given the huge diversity of music therapy training programmes in Europe, and the ever-changing music therapy landscape, the selection of ten training courses cannot claim to be representative or comprehensive. Yet, we believe that the selection made here provides a good overview, and may also serve as a starting point for further, more encyclopedic endeavours.

The structure of the book

The second chapter of Part I by Johanna Schmid and Thomas Stegemann – an overview of all music therapy training programmes in Europe – is based on the diploma thesis of the first author, supervised by the head of the Viennese music therapy training course. It provides a synoptic view of the current situation concerning music therapy education in 45 European Countries – from Albania to the United Kingdom.

In the second Part of the book, ten selected European music therapy programmes are portrayed following a common framework. Each chapter starts off with the most important information on a one-page *fact sheet*. Alone, by comparing these data, it becomes evident how much music therapy programmes differ in terms of course structure, study periods, target groups, admission requirements, tuition fees, and so on. In the following section, the *theoretical background, the philosophy, and the therapy principles* underlying the concepts of each training course are explained and elaborated. Again, the diversity displayed in this section underlines the rich interdisciplinary context of music therapy – and it might also explain, why it is sometimes so difficult to speak with one voice. *Admission criteria and admission procedures* are addressed in the next section, mirroring the foci of the training programmes with respect to content of the curriculum as well as regarding the formal framework conditions. The third section of each chapter delineates the *structure and content* of the particular training programme. Interestingly, there are some areas that show great similarities – we will comment on this in the last part of this book. The following section picks up on a topic that can be described as the core of every music therapy training programme: *clinical training and internships*. And of course, there would be no music therapy without music – that's why an extra section is dedicated to the *musical training* within the respective curricula.

Further, it is a matter of great importance to us, paying particular attention to the field of *experiential learning and music therapy self-experience*. From our point of view, the way students learn how to reflect on "the things going on in therapy", in relation to the dynamics of personal experiences and the own inner world, is a key aspect of quality in every therapy training. To complete the picture, the last section deals with a topic that is increasingly gaining importance: *the evaluation procedures concerning the quality of teaching*. Finally, if applicable, information on the PhD programme in music therapy is provided.

Part III of the book offers a conclusion and an outlook by the editors, summing up and commenting on the synopsis of curricula depicted in the previous chapters. Short biographies of every contributor can be found in chapter 14. An appendix to chapter 2 (*overview*) provides a table with the main facts to 119 European music therapy programmes.

Theme and variations

The Wikipedia entry to "Variation (music)" reads as follows: "In music, variation is a formal technique where material is repeated in an altered form. The changes may involve harmony, melody, counterpoint, rhythm, timbre, orchestration or any combination of these" (2016). The concept of this book was to give a theme – in the form of a framework, as mentioned above – and to invite music therapists from different European countries to "play" with this framework and to create their own "variation" by adding their particular melody, harmony, orchestration, and so on. In a nod to the EMTC2016's motto, one could even say, that together with the reader "A Symphony of Dialogues" emerges. The aim of this publication is to show both the *theme* (i.e., the common ground) and the *variations* (i.e., the idiosyncratic aspects) of European music therapy education. Paying tribute to diversity as well as to congruence – in a differentiated and respectful manner – seems badly needed in Europe these days. Thus, we hope that this book will make a small contribution to the future development of a European music therapy – in training, research, and practice.

Acknowledgements

First and foremost, we owe special thanks to the contributors who helped to put this book together in time (in alphabetical order): Jos De Backer, Lars Ole Bonde, Ludwika Konieczna, Stine Lindahl Jacobsen, Edith Lecourt, Melissa Mercadal-Brotons, Mirdza Paipare, Katie Roth, Johanna Schmid, Ferdinando Suvini, Luk Van Wuytswinkel, and Tessa Watson.

Furthermore, we would like to thank the president of the European Music Therapy Confederation, Hanne Mette Ridder, as well as Monika Ribaupierre and Karin Schumacher, two music therapy pioneers, for sharing with us their highly valued thoughts and experiences in the forewords to this book.

In addition, we would like to say thank you to Jana Kilbertus for drawing the maps for chapter 2, and to Katharina Pfeiffer for helping with the first layout of the manuscript.

Last but not least we would like to express our gratitude to the Reichert Verlag, in particular to Ursula Reichert who was willing to take the chance of realising this special publication project, and who together with her team took care of this book project – as always – in a very helpful and diligent way.

2 Music therapy training programmes in Europe – an overview

Johanna Schmid and Thomas Stegemann

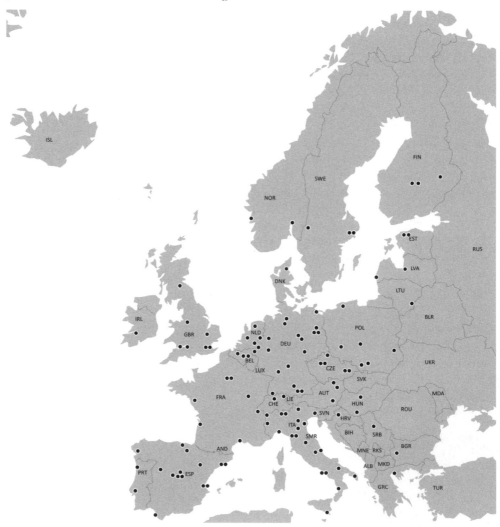

Figure 1: Music Therapy training courses in Europe in 2015, graphic by Jana Kilbertus

1. Introduction

Based on the Viennese diploma thesis "Music Therapy Training Courses in Europe" (Schmid, 2014), this chapter aims to give an overview of music therapy training programmes in Europe. Europe's diversity is reflected in the variety of music therapy courses: short-term courses, bachelor, master, diploma, further education/advanced training programmes and PhD courses. Relating to Karin Reissenberger's (aka Karin Schumacher's) thesis (1970) – which dealt with the topic of music therapeutic efforts within the European area up to the 1970s – it is obvious, that an enormous development of music therapy educational programmes has taken place.

Even in the last 10 years music therapy education in Europe has seen a massive rise. If you take Austria as an example, two of the three music therapy training institutes emerged in the last five years: the bachelor-equivalent course at *Kunstuniversität Graz* was established in 2010, the courses at the IMC *University of Applied Sciences* in Krems started in 2009 (bachelor's course) and 2012 (master's course) (Geretsegger, 2012).

In total, 45 countries[1] are included in the research and divided into five geographic areas: Central Europe, Eastern Europe, Southern and South-Eastern Europe, Western Europe and Northern Europe.

All in all, 119 music therapy training courses are taken into account.

The prevailing research method was web-based field research, mainly through direct or E-Mail contact with the heads of the training programmes, but also with students. By asking them the questions below, it was possible to gain insight about the theoretical background, the tuition fees, the subjects, the duration of the programme and the therapeutic approach.

The following questions were included in the research:

Are the training courses bachelor, master, diploma, or advanced training courses?

How many semesters does the training course take?

Is there an entrance examination? If yes, what does it include?

Which subjects does the programme include?

How much are the tuition/registration/entrance examination fees?

Towards which therapeutic approach/method is the programme oriented?

Important sources of information were also the *European Music Therapy Confederations'* website (www.emtc-eu.com) based on Monika Nöcker-Ribeaupierre's work (2007/2010) and the music therapy online forum *Voices* (www.voices.no).

---

1   Albania, Andorra, Austria, Belarus, Belgium, Bosnia and Herzegovina, Bulgaria, Croatia, Cyprus, Czech Republic, Denmark, Estonia, Finland, France, Germany, Greece, Hungary, Iceland, Ireland, Italy, Latvia, Liechtenstein, Lithuania, Luxembourg, Malta, Moldavia, Monaco, Montenegro, Netherlands, Norway, Poland, Portugal, Republic of Macedonia, Romania, Russia, San Marino, Serbia, Slovakia, Slovenia, Spain, Sweden, Switzerland, Turkey, Ukraine, United Kingdom

2. Music therapy courses in Europe

The map above shows all courses discussed here. As it is not possible to discuss all training courses in this context in detail, one example for each geographic region will be presented. The examples are chosen by chance and not for any particular reason. Further informations in English language can be found in the thesis "Music Therapy training courses in Europe" (Schmid, 2014).

The presentation of the courses follows their location according to five European geographic areas, as proposed by the "Ständiger Ausschuss für geographische Namen (StAGN)". These areas are:

- Central Europe
- Eastern Europe
- Southern and South-Eastern Europe
- Western Europe
- Northern Europe[2]

---

2   Note: This categorisation is different from the EMTC's organisational structure, dividing Europe in three regions (North, Middle, and South).

3. Music therapy courses in Central Europe

Figure 2: Music therapy courses in Central Europe, graphic by Jana Kilbertus

The following countries in Central Europe were researched for offering music therapy programmes:

- Austria (AUT)
- Croatia (HRV)
- Czech Republic (CZE)
- Estonia (EST)
- Germany (DEU)
- Hungary (HUN)
- Latvia (LVA)
- Liechtenstein (LIE)
- Lithuania (LTU)
- Luxembourg (LUX)
- Poland (POL)
- Slovakia (SVK)
- Slovenia (SVN)

- Switzerland (CHE)

Switzerland was chosen here as an example.

According to the SFMT (Schweizerischer Fachverband für Musiktherapie), in French: ASMT (Association Professionelle Suisse de Musicothérapie), five institutes offer training programmes in Switzerland – all programmes are privately run, except the MAS Klinische Musiktherapie at the Zürcher Hochschule der Künste (ZHdK) (SMFT/ASMT, 2013), which is also the only master's course.

Zürcher Hochschule der Künste (ZHdK) Zürich

The Zürcher Hochschule der Künste (ZHdK) offers three different programmes (Deutsche Musiktherapeutische Gesellschaft [DMtG], 2015, p. 126ff):

a.   Master of Advanced Studies (MAS) in clinical music therapy

b.   Further education in music psychotherapy

c.   Upgrade Master of Advanced Studies (MAS) for professionally trained music therapists

3.a. MAS in clinical music therapy

The training programme takes four years. Candidates need to have completed a study in either music, special education, psychology, pedagogy, social work or medicine. In addition, clinical or therapeutic work experience, musical and improvisational practice, 40 hours of music therapeutic group self-experience, and 20 hours of individual therapy are obligatory.

The entrance examination consists of a face-to-face interview, including a musical-improvisational dialogue, singing and accompanying a song, trio improvisation and reflections.

Fees for the course are: 200 CHF (~180 €; all amounts based on exchange rates of April 30, 2016) registration fee, 500 CHF (~455 €) for the admission procedure, 3,800 CHF (~3,460 €) tuition fee per semester, and 1,600 CHF (~1,457 €) examination fee (S. Lutz Hochreutener, personal communication, April 28, 2016). Approximate total: 32,700 CHF (~29,790 €).

The course consists of different modules, including subjects such as "General methodology of music therapy", "Theory of music therapy", "Training in scientific working", "Psychology", "Psychopathology", "Individuaul training music therapy", "Improvisation", "Supervision", etc.

Two internships (altogether 300 hours) and at least 120 hours of independent clinical music therapeutic professional practice are required.

The programme's orientation is towards the humanistic mainstream, but integrates also depth psychology, learning theory and systemic approaches (DMtG, 2015, p. 128, translated by the authors).

3.b. Further education in music psychotherapy

This training takes five or six years and consists of four years of clinical music therapy training and one to two years for the upgrade in clinical music therapy (DMtG, 2015, p. 130ff). The graduates' title in music-psychotherapy is recognised by the Swiss Charta for Psychotherapy.

The requirements for the entrance exam, the therapeutic orientation and the costs for the training are as stated in 3.a.

Subjects include "Indication and Contraindication", "Assessment and indication specific interventional practice", "Supervision" etc. (DMtG, 2015, p. 131).

300 hours of internships and two years of psychotherapeutic practice in a psychiatric, medical, psychotherapeutic or psychosocial institution are included in the training (DMtG, 2015, p. 132, translated by the authors).

3.c. MAS for professionally trained music therapists

This Master of Advanced Studies (MAS) programme is designed for music therapists who want to expand their professional knowledge, it takes 2,5 years (depending on former educational qualification) (DMtG, 2015, p. 134ff).

Candidates need to have a diploma in music therapy, and need to have at least 120 hours of music therapeutic practical experience per year after graduating in music therapy, 20 hours of further training per year, 20 hours of supervision per year, and 50 hours music therapy self-experience (S. Lutz Hochreutener, personal communication, April 28, 2016).

The entrance exam consists of an application. Fees for the course include 200 CHF (~180 €) registration fee, tuition fee 5,400 CHF (at maximum) (~ 4,917 €), and 1,600 CHF (~1,457 €) examination fee (S. Lutz Hochreutener, personal communication, April 28, 2016). Subjects are for example "Methods of music therapy", "Research in music therapy", "Developmental psychology" (DMtG, 2015, p. 135, translated by the authors). The therapeutic orientation is integrative with a focus on humanistic approaches (as stated above).

4. Music therapy courses in Eastern Europe

Figure 3: Music therapy courses in Eastern Europe, graphic by Jana Kilbertus

The research included
- Belarus (BLR)
- Russia (RUS)
- Ukraine (UKR)

Currently there are no established training courses, though there used to be a continuing education programme in Orenburg (Russia), which was a cooperation between the Hochschule für Musik und Theater Hamburg, the L. and M. Rostropovich-University for Music and Fine Arts and the Psychotherapeutic Centre Orenburg. In 2016, the second class will start there (H.-H. Decker-Voigt, personal communication, June 28, 2015).

From 2000 the Faculty of Social Pedagogy and Psychology at the State University of Zaporizhzhya has cooperated with the Faculty of Music Therapy of the University of Applied Sciences Magdeburg-Stendal and has offered a music therapy module (Ivannikova, 2002). Yet, active cooperation has ended now.

5. Music therapy courses in Southern and South-Eastern Europe

Figure 4: Music therapy courses in Southern and South-Eastern Europe, graphic by Jana Kilbertus

The following Southern and South-Eastern countries were included in the research for music therapy programmes:

- Albania (ALB)
- Andorra (AND)
- Bosnia and Herzegovina (BIH)
- Bulgaria (BGR)
- Greece (GRC)
- Cyprus (CYP)
- Italy (ITA)
- Malta (MLT)
- Moldavia (MDA)
- Monaco (MCO)
- Montenegro (MNE)

- Portugal (PRT)
- Republic of Macedonia (MKD)
- Romania (ROU)
- San Marino (SMR)
- Serbia (SRB)
- Spain (ESP)
- Turkey (TUR)

Portugal was chosen as an example. At the moment there are two music therapy training programmes in Portugal, both at graduate level (European Music Therapy Confederation [EMTC] 2011-2015, date of access: August 31, 2015).

Universidade Lusíada de Lisboa (Lissabon)

The programme is a master's programme (120 ECTS), takes four semesters and is designed after American education models (Fundaçao Minerva – Cultura – Ensino e Investigaçao Cientifica / Universidades Lusiada, 2004 – 2011).

Students who want to apply need to have a bachelor's degree, or an appropriate CV that enables them to carry out the study (Fundaçao Minerva – Cultura – Ensino e Investigaçao Cientifica / Universidades Lusiada, 2004 – 2011).

According to the blog "Musicoterapia en Portugal" the registration fees are 250 €, the tuition fees 4,000 €.

Subjects are for example "Psychopathology", "Improvisation in music therapy", "Psychology of health", and "Methodology of intervention" (Fundaçao Minerva – Cultura – Ensino e Investigaçao Cientifica / Universidades Lusiada, 2004 – 2011, translated by the author).

6. Music therapy courses in Western Europe

Figure 5: Music therapy courses in Western Europe, graphic by Jana Kilbertus

Western Europe has courses in these countries to offer:

- Belgium (BEL)
- France (FRAU)
- Ireland (IRL)
- Netherlands (NLD)
- United Kingdom (GBR)

As the United Kingdom accommodates one of the oldest music therapy training courses in Europe, the UK was chosen as a representative for Western Europe.

Guildhall School of Music and Drama (London)

The *Guildhall School of Music and Drama* offers a two-year master's programme.

The general entrance requirements are: high standard of musicianship, a mature personality and graduate level academic skills (Guildhall School of Music and Drama, 2015). Candidates have to prepare two pieces on their first instrument, one piece on the second instrument, a short piece for unaccompanied voice (such as a folk song). Furthermore, they have to accomplish some sight-singing, free improvisation, simple keyboard harmonies and interactive improvisation at the audition (Guildhall School of Music and Drama, 2015). Additionally, there is an interview with the head of music therapy as well as an external psychotherapist.

The total costs for the course are 14,670 £ (=17,407.50 €) for UK/EU students and 33,350 £ (=39,573.30 €) for non-EU-students (Guildhall School of Music and Drama, 2015).

There are several modules (for example "Clinical practice and reflection 1" or "Applied theoretical and research studies"). Subjects are for example "Music therapy theory and literature seminar", "Keyboard improvisation", "Personal therapy" and "Music therapy techniques", including three clinical placements (Guildhall School of Music and Drama, 2015).

The programme is influenced by a psychodynamic approach (Guildhall School of Music and Drama 2015).

7. Music therapy courses in Northern Europe

Figure 6: Music therapy courses in Northern Europe, graphic by Jana Kilbertus

In Northern Europe the following countries were included in the research:

* Denmark (DNK)
* Finland (FIN)
* Iceland (ISL)
* Norway (NOR)
* Sweden (SWE)

Norway was taken as an example.

Norwegian Academy of Music (Oslo)

The bachelor's programme in Oslo consists of one year of study of music and health (60 ECTS), after an undergraduate degree (120 ECTS) (Trondalen, Rolvsjord, Stige, 2010). After these three years, students can do two years of full time training to complete the master level (120 ECTS) (Trondalen, Rolvsjord, Stige, 2010). There is also a PhD programme (180 ECTS).

There are entrance exams to both the bachelor and the master level, consisting of musical tasks and an interview (G.Trondalen, personal communication, September 18, 2013).

The Norwegian government pays for education: there are no fees.

Subjects are "Self experience", "Music therapy theory", "Clinical practice with supervision" and "Research methodology" (G.Trondalen, personal communication, September 18, 2013).

The approach the Norwegian Academy of Music follows, is eclectic: there are humanistic, developmentally and cultural theories, there's also an influence of Nordoff-Robbins and a focus on improvisation (G.Trondalen, personal communication, September 18, 2013).

8. References

Deutsche Musiktherapeutische Gesellschaft (Ed.). (2015). *Studien- und Ausbildungslandschaft Musiktherapie 2015* [Music therapy training programmes 2015] (14th ed.). Berlin: Deutsche Musiktherapeutische Gesellschaft.

European Music Therapy Confederation (EMTC). (2015). *Training Courses: Portugal.* Available from: EMTC website, www.emtc-eu.com

Geretsegger, M. (2012). Music therapy in Austria. *Proceedings of Bridging Nations and Ideas: 2012 World Music Therapy Association Presidential Reports at the Seoul Summit Meeting* (pp. 43-53). Seoul, Korea: Korean Music Therapy Association.

Guildhall School of Music and Drama. (2015). *MA in Music Therapy.* Available from: Guildhall School of Music and Drama website, http://www.gsmd.ac.uk

Ivannikova, M. (2002, November). Music therapy in the Ukraine. *Voices: A World Forum for Music Therapy.* Retrieved March 24, 2014, from http://www.voices.no/country/monthukraine_nov2002.html

Musicoterapia en Portugal. (2006, March 4). *Formación de Máster en Musicoterapia en Lisboa (Portugal).* [Blog post]. Retrieved from http://musicoterapiaenportugal.blogia.com

Reissenberger, K. (1970). *Versuch einer Überschau musiktherapeutischer Bemühungen innerhalb des europäischen Raumes* [Attempt of an overview of music therapeutic efforts within the European area]. Unpublished diploma thesis, Akademie für Musik und darstellende Kunst Wien, Vienna.

Schmid, J. (2014). *Music Therapy Training Courses in Europe.* Unpublished diploma thesis, Universität für Musik und darstellende Kunst Wien, Vienna.

Ständiger Ausschuss für geografische Namen (StAGN). (n.d.). In *Wikipedia.* Retrieved February 22, 2016 from https://de.wikipedia.org/wiki/Ständiger_Ausschuss_für_geographische_Namen

Trondalen, G., Rolvsjord, R. ,& Stige, B. (2010, July). Music therapy in Norway – approaching a new decade. *Voices Resources.* Retrieved March 18, 2014, from http://testvoices.uib.no/community/?q=country-of-the-month/2010-music-therapy-norway-approaching-new-decade

3 Vienna, Austria

Thomas Stegemann and Elena Fitzthum

©Mischa Erben

©Irmgard Bankl

Department for Music Therapy
University of Music and Performing Arts Vienna
www.mdw.ac.at/mbm/mth

Full time Music Therapy Programme

University of Music and Performing Arts Vienna, AUT

FACT SHEET

Institution:	University of Music and Performing Arts Vienna, Austria
Programme Head:	Univ.-Prof. Dr. med. Dr. sc. mus. Thomas Stegemann
Study Period:	8 semesters
ECTS Credits:	240
Number of students:	10 per year
Teaching personnel capacities:	C3 Professorship, Research Assistant (0.5 FTE), Secretary, Lectureships
Tuition Fee:	None (for citizens of EU member states); ÖH membership fee of € 18.70
Target Group/ Addressees:	High-school graduates
Admission Requirements:	Qualification for university entrance and admission examination (if German is not the first language, proof of German skills is required in addition)
Language of Instruction:	German
Type:	Full time Programme (equivalent to integrated master's degree)
Academic Degree:	Magister/Magistra artium (Mag./Mag.ᵃ)
Occupational Title:	Music Therapist (full responsibility according to Austrian music therapy law)
Others:	PhD Programme (see p. 45)

The following link provides further information: www.mdw.ac.at/mbm/mth

1. Background: Developments, theories, and philosophy

In 1959, the first Austrian music therapy training course was founded at what was then the Vienna Academy of Music (today: University of Music and Performing Arts Vienna). With respect to the long tradition, making Austria one of the pioneering countries for music therapy in Europe, and in recognition of the distinct psychotherapeutic orientation, the term '*Wiener Schule der Musiktherapie*' (Viennese School of Music Therapy) was coined.

Today, the Viennese School of Music Therapy can be understood as a tradition of teaching music therapy that has been empirically developed from the clinical work – in particular, in paediatrics, psychiatry, and psychosomatics – and that is informed both by a humanistic and psychodynamic approach. Free improvisation – with its communicative potential – is at the heart of the music therapy methods applied on the Viennese training course (Stegemann, 2014).

In order to better understand the concept of the Viennese School of Music Therapy, it is crucial to acknowledge three main sources which have been highly influential for the development of the Viennese training course: (1) clinical background, (2) humanistic approach, and (3) influences from psychotherapy schools.

(1) The clinical background is closely connected with the historical development of music therapy in Austria: Editha Koffer-Ullrich, the founder of the Viennese training course, was a highly talented violinist, who graduated in the 1920s from the Viennese Academy of Music and Performing Arts with distinction ("mit Auszeichnung"). Later, she spent seven years in Tanzania. Those years in Africa had a huge impact on her thinking about music as she became acquainted with healing rituals and the 'exotic music' of Africa, in particular with the powerful rhythms of African tribal music. Thus, she became interested in music therapy. To learn more about music therapy – at that time practically unknown in Austria – she went to the USA, where music therapy was already practiced in various hospitals along the east coast. Back in Vienna – thanks to her excellent contacts within the Viennese high society, including renowned physicians like Hans Hoff and Andreas Rett, as well as Hans Sittner, director of the Viennese Academy of Music – she managed to establish the first academic music therapy training course on the European continent in 1959. Her 'vision', as she wrote one year earlier, was about to come true:

Vienna, through a long tradition closely affiliated with medicine and music, is called to make a special contribution [to the development of music therapy]. In our hometown, for the benefit of the suffering people, both disciplines [medicine and music] shall act together in theory and practice, in hospital and in research. (Koffer-Ullrich, 1958 as cited in Mössler, 2008, p. 19)

From the very beginning, clinical placements – at first in paediatrics, 'Kinderklinik Lainz' (Prof. Rett) – were inherent parts of the curriculum. Medical doctors, like Hoff and colleagues, were fascinated by the idea, that music therapy might open a new – a non-verbal – way of getting in contact with the patients. Thus, the new music therapy training course at the Viennese Academy of Music was, at the same time, the initiation of clinical music therapy in Austria as the so-called *Sonderlehrgang Musikheilkunde* (extraordinary music therapy training course) run parallel to the first steps of music therapy pioneers in Viennese hospitals. The pioneers of the first generation of music therapy teachers – besides Koffer-Ullrich, Ilse Castelliz, Alfred Schmölz, and Albertine Wesecky, to name but a few – were connected through a similar approach to music therapy which was characterised by understanding man as a creative being focusing on active use of musical parameters in music therapy aiming to motivate the patients to foster expressiveness and communication. (Mössler, 2008, p. 230)

In addition, the concept of harmony – based on Pythagorean theory, and refined by Hans Kayser in the 20th century – played a major role within in the Viennese School of Music Therapy; in particular, as the only university chair worldwide for theoretical research on harmony (*Harmonikale Grundlagenforschung*) was located at the University of Music and Performing Arts Vienna, Austria.

(2) In 1970, Alfred Schmölz became the head of the Viennese music therapy training course which he was going to lead for not less than 22 years. Schmölz was a piano teacher who was influenced by the teachings of Heinrich Jacoby, a music teacher and a proponent of the progressive educational movement (Fitzthum, 2003). Jacoby refused to accept the dichotomy of "musical" vs. "unmusical" – instead, he declared that music should be considered a means of expression not different from language. Thus, music is ubiquitous and there is no such thing as "being unmusical". Furthermore, Jacoby – who read Freud, and maintained contact with Alfred Adler – integrated influences from psychodynamic therapy schools into his educational approach. In particular, he stressed the importance of free improvisation – in contrast to only reproducing music. These humanistic and psychodynamic ideas were highly influential on Schmölz' way of thinking. Working in psychosomatics as a music therapist, he introduced and integrated these concepts into his own music therapy approach. Certain improvisation tasks that are attributed to Schmölz are still part of the techniques that are taught students today, i.e. *Paukenpartnerspiel* (playing a dialogue on a timpani), or *Einzeltonspiel am Klavier* (playing a dialogue on the piano with the restriction of only playing one note at a time). Thus, the music therapist's stance – according to the understanding of the Viennese tradition of music therapy – is very much coined by the humanistic philosophy and the spirit of the reform movement (Fitzthum, 2003).

(3) According to Mössler's historical model of the development of the Viennese training course (2008), the era of the pioneers was followed by the second generation. The latter is characterised by music therapists who completed – in addition to the Viennese training course – a training in psychotherapy. Amongst others, Elena Fitzthum, Dorothea Oberegelsbacher, and Dorothee Storz are representatives of this generation, who are still in charge today. Although the psychotherapy schools were different (e.g., gestalt therapy, individual psychology, system-

ic therapy) within the psychodynamic approach – combined with a humanistic background – they found common ground. The strong connection to psychotherapy, in particular influenced the self-conception of the second generation's music therapists as being "therapists" – in contrast to being the doctor's musical auxiliaries. This paved the way for the introduction of music therapy self-experience as a compulsory part of the curriculum in the 1990s. On the downside, the focus on psychotherapeutic methods and techniques led to a development where the music was at risk of fading into the background. Meanwhile, this tendency has levelled off, and the awareness of the importance of music as such in music therapy has risen again.

In summary, Viennese music therapy with its psychotherapeutic identity is characterised by a humanistic and psychodynamic approach. In its clinical orientation, and with respect to the therapeutic stance, it is strongly shaped by the traditional areas of practice, i.e. psychiatry, psychosomatics, and child and adolescent psychiatry.

2. Admission criteria and admission procedures

The admission requirements for the diploma studies in music therapy at the University of Music and Performing Arts Vienna encompass an upper secondary school leaving exam and the successful admission examination.

Admission to this full-time study programme also requires that the applicant's command of the German language corresponds to at least C1 level. As documentation of this, the following diplomas are accepted: a C1 diploma from an ÖSD testing centre (Oberstufe Deutsch) or one from a Goethe Institute testing centre (Goethe-Zertifikat C1).

In addition to the usual documents that have to be handed in for the registration of the admission examination (CV and certificates), it is mandatory to provide a personal statement regarding one's own motivation to become a music therapist as well as ideas and expectations with respect to the profession of a music therapist. Further, it is strongly recommended to provide evidence of self-experience in music therapy, and first experiences with internships in music therapy practice.

The 3-day admission examination basically consists of a musical part (2 days) and the music therapy part (1 day) – besides a language test on the first day for students whose mother tongue is not German.

Musical skills

Overall, the requirements for the level of musical skills and talent are guided by the criteria that apply for the admission examination of music education. This includes a written test in music theory and ear training (for example, you have to notate rhythms, or to identify intervals played on the piano).

After successfully completing music theory and ear training, instrumental and vocal skills are examined in several auditions to check the candidates for musical talent, flexibility, capability, and experience. Basic skills in piano and guitar playing are mandatory, in addition the mastery of a melody instrument (e.g. flute) and vocal skills are required. Since 2014, there is an additional audition for the candidates' main musical instrument to assure a certain level of virtuosity as the students will receive two years of one-to-one lessons in this subject to further develop their own musical and artistic identity.

Overview of the musical parts of the admission examination and examples of the requirements

(1) PIANO

- performance of two pieces from two different epochs; level of difficulty: e.g. Bach (two-part inventions); Sonatinas or easy Sonatas; Bartók/Mikrokosmos, Volume 2 and 3 etc.
- Harmonic cadences in major and minor in different keys (up to three accidentals) in different positions/inversions.
- accompaniment: to a given melody (chart) the candidate has to play the proper chords (I-IV-V).

(2) VOCALS (sight-singing) and singing with accompaniment

- sight-singing (easy melodies in ascending difficulty)
- singing songs with guitar accompaniment by heart (the candidate has to prepare 10 songs from which two or three will be chosen by the examining board; easy folk tunes, lullabies, pop songs etc.)
- singing songs with piano accompaniment by heart (see above)

(3) MELODY INSTRUMENT

- to play songs by heart with improvised introduction/prelude and outro/postlude (can be chosen from the same list as for the vocal test).
- to transpose the songs into different keys (up to three accidentals)
- performance of two musical pieces (with or without accompaniment)

(4) MAIN MUSICAL INSTRUMENT

- As main musical instrument all instruments can be chosen that are taught at the university (classical music as well as pop music).
- The requirements are determined by the professors of the respective musical instrument.
- Example: Saxophone (popular music) requires "sufficient technical skills in playing the instrument, and basic knowledge in popular music";
- performance of three pop music pieces of medium difficulty (blues, easy listening, pop tune, jazz etude, etc.) with or without playalong.
- an easy jazz etude (Niehaus, Snidero, …)
- All scales in major and minor

Every single part of the admission examination has to be passed to proceed to the next step.

Music therapy skills

After passing the musical part of the admission examination, the candidates are admitted to the music therapy part on the third day. While during the first two days there are mainly music teachers in the examination board, the tests and the interview on the third days are conducted by music therapists.

The practical parts focus on improvisation and communication/interaction:

(1) IMPROVISATION SOLO (8-10 min.)
- the candidates are invited to freely improvise to an abstract painting (the candidates are allowed to choose one picture from a series of paintings provided).
- They can choose to use one or more musical instruments and/or their voice (the choice of musical instruments include the "typical" music therapy instruments as Orff instruments, percussion, piano, etc.)
- After the improvisation the candidates are asked to reflect on the improvisation and on their feelings and thoughts during the music.

(2) MUSICAL INTERACTION (8-10 min.)
- The candidate is asked to do a free improvisation together with one member from the examination board to a given situation (e.g., argument between siblings, trying to come in contact with a patient suffering from depression).
- After the musical interaction the candidates are asked to reflect on the improvisation and on their feelings and thoughts during the music.

(3) GROUP IMPROVISATION (45 min.)
- In groups of ten candidates different improvisational tasks in the group setting are explored (e.g. free improvisation, taking turns)
- The candidates are asked to reflect on the interaction in the group, and their own role within the group improvisation.

(4) INTERVIEW

Finally, there is a short interview with every candidate and the examination board (5-10 min.). During this interview candidates will be asked how they have experienced the admission examination so far, why they are interested in studying music therapy, and what they expect from becoming a music therapist. This interview also offers the opportunity to clarify and answer other questions, e.g. regarding organisational aspects of the training course.

In summary, outstanding and multi-faceted musical skills are a prerequisite for the admission. In addition, individual qualifications and aptitude to become a music therapist are checked/considered carefully. The structure and the content of the music therapy part derive from the experiences made in music therapy practice, relating to the challenges of working as a music therapist, and to the psychotherapeutic approach of the training course. Working as a music therapist means bearing responsibility for the clients/patients, and to deal with the demands of a multi-professional setting. Thus, the music therapist is challenged as an individual and personhood, in particular with respect to their social and communicative skills. The free musical improvisation with clients/patients – in individual therapy or in group therapy – requires a high level of empathy as well as a well-balanced regulation of closeness and distance in professional relationships. Although the development of these skills will be a key point during the training course – both in music therapy self-experience and in music therapy internships – a certain degree of personal maturity and reflective faculty can be considered a prerequisite for entering the music therapy training course.

Due to the limited capacities of one-to-one music lessons and internships places, only 10 students are enrolled every year.

3. Structure and content of the curriculum

General information concerning legal regulations in Austria

The degree that students receive after successfully completing the music therapy training course in Vienna entitles them to be registered as a Music Therapist with full responsibility according to legal regulations. In Austria, music therapy has been regulated as a healthcare profession by the Austrian Music Therapy Law since July 1, 2009 (http://www.oebm.org/files/musiktherapiegesetz.pdf). Regarding the structure and content of music therapy training curricula in Austria, the Music Therapy Law so far only provides a framework, outlining the general principles as follows:

> (2) The training course must encompass all essential theoretical and practical contents that are required in order to work in all conscience as a music therapist; including the acquisition of clinical skills and experiences with due regard being given to the basic scientific knowledge in clinical psychology, medicine, and psychotherapy. (MuthG, 2008, p. 5; translation by TS)

The only subjects that are explicitly required by law are (the number of units refer to the degree with full responsibility, i.e. diploma or master level):

- self-experience (200 units; 1 unit = 45 min.)
- vocational and legal studies (60 units)
- ethical aspects in music therapy (60 units)

At the time of writing this chapter (January 2016), a commission (composed of members of the Ministry of Health, of the two professional associations, and heads of the music therapy training programmes) has just started to define obligatory training regulations, supplementary to the Austrian music therapy law (MuthG § 11).

Structure and content of the music therapy diploma studies in Vienna (mdw)

The music therapy training course is an 8 semester (4 years) full-time curriculum, encompassing 240 ECTS-credits.

It includes theoretical and practical lessons, internships, as well as self-experience (individual and group setting).

Key areas of study include:

1. Music Therapy Core
2. Medical and Psychological Basics
3. Musical Education

Curriculum Overview: Year 1

Music Therapy Core

- Lecture Series Music Therapy ("Ringvorlesung", overview of music therapy history, methods, and fields of occupation)
- Basics of Music Therapy ("Praxeologie", including methods and techniques)
- History and Methods of Music Therapy (lecture)
- Body experience/Music and Movement
- Proseminar Child and Adolescent Psychiatry
- Self-experience (individual and group setting)

Medical and Psychological Basics

- Biology, Anatomy, and Physiology (lecture)
- Psychiatry (lecture)
- Developmental Psychology
- Introduction to Psychology
- Neurobiological Fundamentals
- Introduction to Psychotherapy 1

Musical Education

- Voice Training
- Music Theory and Analysis
- Percussion
- Improvisation (piano)
- Choral Conduction/Band Training
- Instrumental or Singing Lesson (one-to-one)

Curriculum Overview: Year 2

Music Therapy Core

- Basics of Music Therapy ("Praxeologie", including methods and techniques)
- Body experience/Music and Movement
- Child and Adolescent Psychiatry (clinical training, seminar, and supervision)
- Proseminar Psychosomatics/Proseminar Psychiatry
- Self-experience (individual and group setting)
- Vocational and Legal Studies

Medical and Psychological Basics

- Research Training 1
- Child and Adolescent Psychiatry (lecture)
- Psychosomatics (lecture)
- Introduction to Psychotherapy 2
- Counselling Techniques

Musical Education

- Improvisation (piano)
- Guitar Lesson
- Instrumental or Singing Lesson (one-to-one)

Curriculum Overview: Year 3

Music Therapy Core

- Basics of Music Therapy ("Praxeologie", including methods and techniques)
- Psychiatry (clinical training, seminar, and supervision)
- Psychosomatics (clinical training, seminar, and supervision)
- "Electives", Clinical Training in different Fields (for details, see section 4)
- Self-experience (individual and group setting)

Medical and Psychological Basics

- Research Training 2

Musical Education

- Group Improvisation Workshop
- Speech Training

Curriculum Overview: Year 4

Music Therapy Core

- Case presentation (music therapy)
- "Electives", Clinical Training in different Fields (for details, see section 4)
- Self-experience (individual)
- Writing the Diploma Thesis (seminar)
- Music and altered states of consciousness
- Ethical Aspects in Music Therapy

Musical Education

- Group Improvisation Workshop
  Note: During the 4th year the students have to write their diploma thesis.

After completing the diploma thesis, the students can take the final exam. The commission-evaluated diploma examination consists of three parts:

- The first part is comprised of the final examinations of all the courses taken as part of this programme.
- The second part consists of a defence of one's academic diploma thesis.
- The third part is a case presentation, focusing on the methods and techniques employed as part of the music therapy treatment process.

4. Clinical training, internships

The music therapy internships – the clinical training at different work places of music therapists – are at the heart of the programme. As outlined in section 1, music therapy internships in hospitals all over Vienna were a constitutive element of the Viennese training course from the very beginning, and the close connection to clinical work in child and adolescent psychiatry, psychiatry, and psychosomatics has had a lasting effect on the development of the Viennese music therapy approach. The focus on mental health, together with the scholarly exchange with leading medical doctors of the time (Rett, Ringel, Hoff, Hartmann to name but a few), and – last not least – the influence of Alfred Schmölz, who coined the term "Viennese School of Music Therapy", has led to the distinct psychotherapeutic orientation of the training course up to the present day.

The clinical training is based on thorough knowledge and skills in music therapy and on fundamental knowledge of medical and psychological basics, acquired during the first year. Internships in child and adolescent psychiatry, psychiatry, and psychosomatics are obligatory for every student (see Curriculum Overview). In addition, at least three more internships in different fields have to be completed by the end of the study. These "electives" can be chosen from the following:

Neonatology, Paediatric Oncology, Special Education, Neurology, Neurorehabilitation, and Geriatrics. Taken together, the music therapy internships add up to a minimum of 765 hours spent at hospitals and schools. Thus, the clinical training alone accounts for approximately 30% of the whole curriculum.

Each of the three mandatory internships (child and adolescent psychiatry, psychiatry, and psychosomatics) is preceded by a "proseminar", i.e. an introductory seminar course over one semester. Aims of the proseminar – given by a music therapist – are an introduction to the working field and the institution where the internship takes place. In addition, it includes information regarding organisation as well as legal and ethical aspects of the respective field of occupation. Further, the students are informed as to how the clinical training will look, and what their duties are. Finally, special exercises, role plays, improvisation tasks etc. will help the students to start the internship well prepared.

The mandatory internships usually take place on one or two days during the semester. Each internship is conducted/run by an experienced music therapist who is paid by the university (sometimes these colleagues also work as a music therapist in the institution where the internships takes place, but in some cases they are only present to supervise the music therapy students). The students learn to work both in an individual setting and in group settings. In any case the internships are accompanied (or paralleled) by supervision on a daily basis, clinical/ward rounds (if possible), and medical seminars. The medical seminars are given by doctors from the institution in order to deepen the students' basic knowledge in medicine and psychology. In supervision and medical seminars there are usually no more than 5 students in the group.

The continuous supervision of the music therapy processes allows for a gradually increasing responsibility of the students with different clients/patients and groups. Ideally, the students have the opportunity to conduct long-term therapies over two semesters. Thus, they can shape and develop their individual "therapy personality" and reflect on psychodynamic processes that only occur during treatments with an established and firm relationship. At the end of the semester, the students have to present their "case", and to write a final report.

5. Musical training

As the Viennese music therapy training course is located at the University of Music and Performing Arts Vienna, outstanding musical skills and talent are considered a prerequisite for enrolment (cf. admission requirements). Based on these musical abilities, the aim of the continuing musical formation is to equip students with comprehensive musical skills on various instruments (including the voice and the body), and to prepare them for the diverse demands of music therapy practice. The development of profound skills in improvisational music is at the core of the curriculum as it builds the bridge to music therapy methods and techniques.

The following classes are mandatory for all students – in addition, the University of Music and Performing Arts Vienna offers a plethora of electives and optional courses ranging from music history and theory classes to ensemble playing, choir singing, or instrument making workshops.

- Improvisation (piano) – 4 semesters
- Group Improvisation Workshop – 4 semesters
- Instrumental or Singing Lesson (one-to-one) – 4 semesters
- Music Theory and Analysis – 2 semesters
- Voice Training – 2 semesters
- Speech Training – 1 semester
- Guitar Lesson (small group) – 2 semesters
- Percussion – 2 semesters
- Choral Conduction/Band Training – 2 semesters

The objective of the improvisation course during the first two years of the curriculum is to provide students with comprehensive practical skills ranging from quite free, unstructured and non-tonal models to much more structured, or directed forms of improvisation. A laboratory spirit of experiment and adventure creates a conducive environment for the confident development of the ability to make spontaneous music, crafted yet free from the potential of preordained form.

Sensitivity to sound and silence, attentive listening, dynamics, motivic differentiation and prolongation techniques together with flexible communicative skills are initially practiced with a core set of instruments within clearly delineated tonal frameworks in small groups, partner improvisations and solos.

Resources are then expanded to encompass the entire pan-chromatic field and to include combinations of dissimilar instruments concurrently with increased emphasis on exchanging and joining together motifs, taking initiative and introducing impulses for transformation. Programmatic improvisatory tasks, including stimuli from the visual arts, provide additional points of departure for musical creation and expand students' aesthetic conception of music and tolerance for the broad spectrum of sounds that constitute music.

During the last two years of the curriculum the emphasis of the improvisation course – now named "Group Improvisation Workshop" – is put on the development of artistic and creative skills, in particular in playing and improvising together in a group setting. Regarding aspects of "mental hygiene", another objective of this course is to help the students to maintain their identity as a musician during a phase of the curriculum when internships, supervision, and scientific work (including the diploma thesis) are predominant and very demanding.

A quite unique feature of the Viennese music therapy training course is the possibility to take one-to-one instrumental or singing lessons over four semesters, referring to one's principal musical instrument (cf. admission examination). Thus, the students are enabled to further develop and optimise their musical skills and their expressiveness with their instrument and/or their voice.

Interestingly, after the musical classes were expanded during the last revision of the curriculum in 2012 (i.e., four instead of two semesters of the Principal Musical Instrument, Guitar Lesson and Group Improvisation Workshop were newly introduced), there has been a significant growth of non-university musical activities, in particular several new band projects.

Music is the music therapist's primary medium. To use music and sounds within a therapeutic relationship, is the unique and specific trait of music therapy in comparison to other approaches – be it other arts therapies, psychotherapy, or music medicine. The aptitude to purposefully use music in a therapy setting not only requires a high degree of empathy and self-reflection, but also the ability to apply musical parameters in a very nuanced and differentiated way. This includes a familiarity with a variety of musical instruments and musical styles, as well as an extensive repertoire of songs from different cultures and different times/epochs. The less a music therapist has to worry about their musical skills, the easier he or she can immerse him/herself into the interpersonal interactions and dynamics of the therapy process.

The overall aim of the musical training is that the student – at the end of the study – has found their own way of integrating the different "personalities" (e.g., as a musician, or as a music teacher) in their identity of a music therapist. The student is able to use music in a spontaneous and flexible way in order to deliberately build and shape a therapeutic relationship – being aware of the limitations and of potential adverse reactions/secondary effects of musical interventions.

6. Experiential learning, music therapy self-experience

In her landmark publication "Ethical thinking in music therapy" (2000) Cheryl Dileo starts the second chapter ("The virtuous music therapist") with the sentence "At the heart of music therapy is the person of the therapist." (p. 27). In particular, in a psychotherapy-oriented music therapy approach, the growth and development of the therapist's personality – including a critical reflexion of one's own beliefs and stances – is considered a crucial element of the curriculum. This may be even more important in a training course, where most of the students enrol more or less right after graduating from high school ("Matura"/"Abitur"). Thus, the guidance and support during a period of adulthood, when students are only beginning to live their "own life", are essential to a working field where students are confronted with the existential aspects of life (be it in neonatology, in hospice care, or in psychiatry with suicidal patients). Working in a therapeutic setting requires a high level of self-reflection and the ability to make precise distinctions between own problems and the patient's problems. Everyone has his or her "blind spots" – as a music therapist it is crucial to be aware of one's own patterns of thinking and to avoid mingling topics from one's own biography with similar but different issues of the patient. This includes learning (by experience) about the mechanisms of transference and countertransference. In summary, to learn more about one's own strengths, limitations, how one appears to other people (a focus of self-experience in a group setting), and – last but not least – how this can be expressed through music, are fundamental aspects of music therapy self-experience. Regarding the didactics of self-experience in the Viennese training course, it is noteworthy that one objective is to reflect on music therapy and psychotherapy methods and techniques applied by the mentor ("Lehrtherapeut"). From time to time (or at the end of the semester), mentor and student will take a look at the therapy process from a meta level to reflect on technical aspects which will help the student to integrate methods and techniques experienced in his/her "own therapy" into their repertoire of skills which can later be drawn upon as a music therapist.

On the Viennese training course, self-experience (individual and group setting) is fully integrated in the curriculum. Self-experience in group setting starts right at the beginning of the study – all 10 students from any given year run together through a music therapy group process of six semesters (180 hours). During the first semester, the students are given the opportunity to choose a music therapist for individual self-experience. Seven mentors ("Lehrtherapeuten") have been entrusted by the university to conduct self-experience and offer interviews to let the students find out what might be a good match for starting a three-year journey together, in addition to accompanying the future music therapist through the ups and downs of the study period. Individual self-experience starts with the second semester and continues on a weekly basis until the seventh semester (90 hours). Thus, music therapy self-experience on the Viennese training course adds up to 270 hours in total (Note: according to the Austrian music therapy law, 200 units of self-experience are mandatory to become a music therapist).

Qualifications of mentors ("Lehrtherapeuten") in self-experience

According to the central role self-experience has within the Viennese music therapy training course, and due to the high degree of responsibility that is inherent in this "therapy-like" setting, the standards and the prerequisites required to work as a mentor ("Lehrtherapeut") include the following: 1) mentors have to hold a licence both as a music therapist and as a psychotherapist (a specialisation in teaching self-experience would be considered as equivalent to a psychotherapy education); 2) several years' experience as a music therapist, including experience in working with adults in addition to working with groups (the latter is only required for self-experience in group setting); 3) to prevent dual relationships in terms of being a teacher (evaluating students) and a mentor ("Lehrtherapeut") at the same time, educators in self-experience must not be a member of the teaching staff. Thus, confidentiality of the contents and processes in self-experience are ensured.

7. Evaluation procedures concerning quality of teaching

At the University of Music and Performing Arts Vienna a teaching evaluation – encompassing music education and music therapy – was initially introduced in 2012. Apart from this official evaluation, many teachers in music therapy have, until now, used ad-hoc questionnaires and group discussions to receive feedback/information regarding their teaching from the students. In the summer semester of 2016, a new evaluation round will start – it is planned to repeat the evaluation every five years.

The current evaluation procedure includes a paper-pencil or – alternatively – an online questionnaire to be filled in by the students for every class. The survey and the evaluation are anonymous. Teachers will receive a summary of the results only from classes where there are more than five students to preserve confidentiality. The format of the survey is adapted to the type of class (e.g., one-to-one lessons, seminars, lectures), consisting of rating questions (Likert scale) and open-ended questions. The evaluation refers to general aspects of the class (including organisation, room, punctuality) as well as questions regarding the style and quality of the teaching, interpersonal dealings (e.g., "I feel I am treated in a fair and respectful manner."), and the impact of the class for future occupational life.

8. PhD Programme

In 2013, the first Austrian PhD programme in music therapy commenced at the University of Music and Performing Arts Vienna – with currently four PhD students at the time of writing this chapter (January 2016).

Admission criteria and structure of the curriculum:

Completion of an academic or artistic diploma or Magister / MA programme, or of a teaching degree programme in accordance with the Austrian legislation AHStG, UniStG or UG, or of a diploma programme in accordance with the KHStG insofar as the subject matter studied is sufficiently related to one of the academic disciplines available at the mdw.

Admission to this full-time study programme also requires the applicant's command of the German language correspond to at least C1 level. As evidence of this, the following diplomas are accepted: a C1 diploma from an ÖSD testing centre (Oberstufe Deutsch) or one from a Goethe Institute testing centre (Goethe-Zertifikat C1).

This course of study consists of two phases that last 2 and 4 semesters respectively.

The first phase concludes with an examination on one's research proposal and related content (individual subject examination); the second phase concludes with a public defence of one's dissertation.

Following completion of this doctoral programme, students receive the academic title "Doctor of Philosophy" ("PhD").

9. References

Dileo, C. (2000). *Ethical thinking in music therapy*. Cherry Hill: Jeffrey Books.

Fitzthum, E. (2003). *Von den Reformbewegungen zur Musiktherapie: Die Brückenfunktion der Vally Weigl. Wiener Beiträge zur Musiktherapie* [From the reform movements to music therapy: Vally Weigl's bridging function. Viennese contributions to music therapy] (Vol. 5). Vienna: Edition Praesens.

Mössler, K. (2008). *Wiener Schule der Musiktherapie: Von den Pionieren zur Dritten Generation. Wiener Beiträge zur Musiktherapie* [Viennese school of music therapy: From the pioneers to the third generation. Viennese contributions to music therapy] (Vol. 8). Vienna: Praesens.

Stegemann, T. (2014). Musiktherapie – mehr als eine Vision [Music therapy – more than just a vision]. In T. Stegemann & E. Fitzthum (Eds.), *Festschrift. 55 Jahre Musiktherapie-Ausbildung an der Universität für Musik und darstellende Kunst Wien* (pp. 125-131). Vienna: University of Music and Performing Arts Vienna.

4 Leuven, Belgium

Jos De Backer and Luk van Wuytswinkel

©Kris Wittevrongel

©Kris Wittevrongel

Music Therapy, academic bachelor and master degree in Music at LUCA, Lemmens campus, Leuven
http://www.luca-arts.be/en/music-therapy-academic-bachelor-degree-and-master-degree-music-lemmens-campus-leuven

Full time BA and MA Music Therapy Programme
LUCA, School of Arts, campus Lemmens, KULeuven, BEL

FACT SHEET

Institution:	LUCA, School of Arts, campus Lemmens, KULeuven
Programme Head:	Prof. Dr. Jos De Backer
Study Period:	6 semesters BA Music Therapy,
	4 semesters MA Music Therapy
ECTS Credits:	180/120 (BA/MA)
Number of students:	Max. 18 per study group
Teaching personnel capacities:	4 professors in Music Therapy (80%, 50%, 40%, 20%),
	2 professors in psychotherapy (100%, 25%),
	7 professors in music improvisation (80%, 60%, 60%, 40%, 60%, 30%, 30%), 8 professors in music (100%, 60%, 50%, 60%, 50%, 50%, 50%, 40%), 2 guest supervisors in music therapy (30%, 30%)
Tuition Fee:	max. 860 €/year (inclusive group music therapy experience and supervision)
Target Group:	Students
Admission Requirements:	Diploma secondary school
Language of Instr.:	Dutch
Type:	Full time BA and MA Programme
Academic Degree:	Bachelor and Master of Music Therapy (BA/MA)
Occupational Title:	MA Music Therapist
Others:	PhD Programme (see p. 58)

The following link provides further information:

http://www.luca-arts.be/en/music-therapy-academic-bachelor-degree-and-master-degree-music-lemmens-campus-leuven

1. Background: Developments, theories, and philosophy

First and foremost, a music therapist is a musician. This does not preclude a focus in psychotherapy, but the candidate should nurture a sincere artistic connection with music and its use in healthcare.

Each candidate's experience with music therapy is unique. What the student does with their training will reflect this. We believe that ideally candidates should be confident in their personal musical tastes and also possess a repertoire for psychotherapeutic training.

Maintaining a distance from the traditional conservatory-style focus on cultivated sounds and expressiveness does not mean giving up technical perfection. For obvious reasons, advanced technical competence is necessary if one is to free oneself from codes of expression that restrict or supress the listener's own responses. It is not essential, however, that students pursue a complete, rigorous musical training in order to cultivate an affinity with a certain kind of practical music making. Before embarking on a career in music therapy, students must confront a disciplined study of music.

The way in which music is handled in a therapeutic setting is embedded in a specific theoretic background. Training programmes differ in their approach to this: the music therapist's we are interested in are psychodynamic, as they are known in the field (De Backer & Sutton, 2014). Our approach applies the principles of psychodynamic training into our own therapeutic method. This framework also has a connection with anthropology, because of a certain vision of humanity. We know that research is not possible without a life science theory; we believe there is a need for a therapeutic, anthropological frame of reference. Without this, theoretical considerations risk being restrictive and could lack the elasticity to be applicable in diverse clinical settings.

We believe the music therapist is a psychotherapist who does not work in a verbal way. The music therapist works at a pre-verbal level, through music. This does not imply, however, that the music therapist does not understand the psychological mechanisms at work. This is because as a therapist they are charged with the care of the patient. The therapist's contribution as a member of a greater team is essential to the effectiveness of the treatment of the patient. He or she also needs to take into consideration the possible utterances of the patient. Undertaking these tasks without an understanding of the underlying psychological mechanisms would be dangerous, as such, a theoretical background is an important component of a music therapist's work. Therefore, students should reach a sufficient intellectual understanding of subjects such as psychopathology, psychiatry and developmental psychology, but also music, and society, depth psychology and so on.

Music as a regressive object gives an obvious and direct access to the emotional world of the patient. Through music, the patients' emotions are expressed. Music is about creating and giving form to that which is without form, or rather has not yet taken form. Essential in this process is the emergence of "moments of synchronicity." Resonance plays a crucial role in this. This is made possible when the music therapist operates with an attitude of empathic listening, or rêverie (De Backer, Foubert & Van Camp, 2014).

Rêverie is a concept introduced by Bion (1967) that refers to the therapist's thinking and attitude while giving form to the chaotic, unbearable world of the patient. During this musical regression it is important that the therapist also goes into a partial state of regression. He or she becomes sensitive to what the patient experiences. In this way, the therapist is closely engaged to the state of the patient, taking cues from each of their senses, according to that of the patient. Moments like these are often concretely visible, as the posture of both therapist and patient respond to a shared sense of pulse. The occurrence of this "resonance" is similar to the relationship between music and dance, or the interplay between movements of the left and right hand; separate, independent elements interact according to a single intention, closely shared between each element. As that moment of synchronicity arrives, the patient's sense of inner self may change, and through improvising can experience the music as an expression coming from within themselves.

2. Admission criteria and admission procedures

Candidates must have a high school diploma and should have at least five years of music lessons in an instrument and/or voice.

The candidate needs to be well-grounded in the field of music as well as in the field of psychotherapy in accordance with the two aspects of the term 'music therapy'. The 'therapy' component functions as the basis for establishing the therapist's role, namely as a therapist. It suggests how the professional identity of the music therapist is not primarily derived from a *conservatoire* style of music education, but rather comes about within her development as a therapist and the socio-professional framework of the mental health care setting in which he or she works.

Candidates should send a portfolio in which is carefully described their musical background, previous education as well as a cover letter discussing their motivation to study music therapy.

Candidates will also take a four-part placement exam:

- Music – dictation of notes and rhythms as typically encountered in classical or popular music; fluent demonstration of playing cadences. Harmonisation of simple melodies on the piano or guitar.
- Instrumental and vocal skills – the performance of a piece of the candidate's choice, of moderate difficulty played on the candidate's primary instrument, or voice.
- Vocal performance of a song
- Free improvisation with a music therapist on piano and percussion and a group improvisation with voice and body percussion.

Finally, we will conduct an individual interview of the candidate to further explore their motivations.

The aim of this test is to gauge the candidate's level of musicality and also if he or she has any experience with improvisation. In addition, candidates will have the opportunity to show their musical imagination, as well as demonstrate how they express themselves verbally.

3. Structure and content of the curriculum

Our programme follows the minimal standards of the European Music Therapy Register (EMTR) and also the minimal standards of the psychotherapeutic profession in Belgium.

Overview of the structure of the programme:

The programme is designed in a three-year (6 semester) Bachelor's programme and a two-year (4 semester) Master's programme.

It is a fulltime training course which means that the students have approximately 20 – 25 contact hours per week for a period of 35 weeks a year.

Additionally, from the third year onwards the students have individual sessions with a professional psychotherapist. This is outside of the programme, but very recommended.

Course contents:

The training course covers advanced knowledge and skills in each artistic and scientific area relevant to the students' future job as a music therapists:

- A knowledge of the most important music therapy repertoire and music as well as scientific and psychodynamic topics
- Training in clinical improvisation
- Knowledge of the most relevant music therapy approaches
- Knowledge of verbal techniques and interventions used in the music therapy profession
- Knowledge of international developments and research in music therapy field
- Insight in musical and therapeutic processes
- Knowledge of the use of music therapy in different fields

Because this is an academic Master's programme, students get experience doing research and are prepared for doctoral studies.

Contents Bachelor in Music Therapy	Contact-hours	Credit points		
		1st	2nd	3 rd
Artistic and musical foundations				
Musical foundations				
Rhythm studies	60	3	3	
Harmonic and melodic ear training	60	6	6	
Melodic and harmonic structure	90	6	6	
Choir and personal project	60	3	3	3
Improvisation and creation				
Instrumental and vocal group improvisation	30	3	3	
Piano or guitar improvisation	30	3		
Piano praxis	30	3	3	
Digital music notation and composition	30	3		
Composition and song-writing	30		3	
Guitar improvisation	30			4
Piano improvisation	30			4
Percussion improvisation	30			4
Melodic improvisation	30			4
Voice improvisation	30			3
Instrumental foundations				
Intro to Guitar	30	3	3	
Intro to Percussion	30	3	3	
Voice	30	3	3	
Ensemble	30	3	3	
Music theoretical foundations				
Music analysis	30			3
Music history	60		3	3
Psychological foundations				
Educational care of people with a mental handicap	30	4		
Developmental psychology	45		5	
Psychodynamic psychology	30			3
Psychiatry and psychopathology	30			3
Music and psyche	30		4	
Introduction in psychotherapy	30	4		

Contents Bachelor in Music Therapy	Contact-hours	Credit points		
		1st	2nd	3 rd
Music therapy foundation				
Introduction in music therapy	30	4		
History of music therapy	15	3		
Music therapeutic play techniques and interventions	30		3	3
Music and handicap	30		3	
Methodology in music therapy	60			4
Self experience in music therapy	30			3
Research in music	30	3		
Research methodology	30		3	
Integrated Bachelor's thesis and presentation				16
Music and handicap: theory and practice; Musical therapeutic play techniques and interventions, clinical improvisation	90			(10)
Music therapy, psychotherapy and literature review	120			(6)
TOTAL of ECTS points		60	60	60

Contents Master in Music Therapy	Contact-hours	Credit points	
		4st	5nd
Artistic and theoretic musical formation			
Guitar improvisation	30	4	
Piano improvisation and clinical improvisation	30	4	4
Percussion improvisation	30	4	
Choir and personal project	30	3	
Music analysis	15	3	3
Melodic improvisation	30	4	
Voice improvisation	30	3	
Ensemble	60		5
Psychological formation			
Music and Psyche; deontology	60	4	
Philosophy and music	30	4	
Child- and Adolescent psychiatry	30	4	
Psychodynamic psychology	30	4	

Contents Master in Music Therapy	Contact-hours	Credit points	
		4st	5nd
Relation and family therapy	30		4
Music therapeutic formation			
Methods of music therapy	60	4	
Music therapeutic play techniques	60	3	
Practicum in music therapy (autism and handicap)	30	3	
Music therapeutic self experience	60	3	
Research methods and literature review	60	6	
Practicum in music therapy (psychiatry)	250		20
Clinical case study	120		14
Master's thesis	90		10
TOTAL of ECTS points		60	60

Further information

Music therapists are trained as professional musicians during the first two years of study. Setting this training within a college of music guarantees that candidates can fully develop their musical skills under the guidance of excellent musicians.

The therapeutic and scientific training runs at two levels: students follow a selection of psychology, psychotherapy and psychiatry courses at the university. A clinical internship takes place within the academic framework of the University Psychiatric Centre, KU Leuven (UPC). At the same time, students get experience in doing scientific research.

In this way, the programme achieves a unique synthesis of artistic and therapeutic professionalism. Courses have been chosen carefully, harmoniously intertwining music, psychotherapy and science.

Beginning from their third year students create their own psychotherapy and music therapy groups. Musical improvisation is emphasized in each of the five instrumental courses (piano, guitar, percussion, voice and a melodic instrument of the student's choice).

4. Clinical training, internships

From the third year on, after being introduced to music therapy in the context of handicapped children, autism and psychotherapy, students will do one group therapy session and one individual session with a child with a handicap or autism. Group sessions meet once per week and have a duration of 45 minutes. The individual session is also once per week with a duration of 40 minutes. The sessions are supervised by an experienced music therapist specialised in treatment of people with special needs.

In the fourth year, the students are asked to lead individual sessions with children demonstrating behavioural disturbances and/or autism. These sessions are also supervised for half an hour per week.

In the fifth year, Masters students will have a fulltime one-year-long internship in a psychiatric hospital or centre for handicap children or adults. The focus is on music therapy as a pre-verbal psychotherapy. The students act as members of a multidisciplinary team, which will demand their responsibility. Weekly, students will have both one-hour-long individual and group supervision with a music therapists and psychotherapist from LUCA or from the centre. Only recognized supervisors (registered as supervisor in the professional association for music therapists, BMT) can take the responsibility for the supervision.

Master students will choose a clinical case study (group or individual) to describe for their final exams and analyse the musical and therapeutic process, the interventions performed, and other relevant information. During the year students will present their progress to an internal and external commission and will be given feedback. The clinical case study will be a part of the master's thesis in which it will connect to theory.

5. Musical training

The musical training of students in music therapy includes the gradual acquisition of skills encompassed in the broad field that is music. This includes learning how to play various musical instruments, a standard practice in the profession. The focus during this training is musical and clinical improvisation. From the start, students are given practical musical assignments and projects to complete independently, with each other, with the listener and at a later stage with patients.

The standard curriculum during the first two years of the artistic musical study includes rhythmic and harmonic ear training as well as the understanding and dealing with melodic and harmonic structures, based on current performed music (classical music, pop, jazz and film music). Students are supported and encouraged as they actively experience the theoretical and, especially, the practical aspects of musical expression. As they develop hands-on skills they give and receive valuable feedback, all within a safe and stimulating environment.

During the first year students improve upon musical studies in piano, guitar, percussion, voice and a melodic instrument. These instrumental studies continue until the first year of the Master's. After developing preliminary technical skills, emphasis is gradually shifted to improvisation. Faculty members are experts in their field and active performers in diverse musical domains like classical, pop, jazz, film music and everything in between.

Performing and improvising in a group setting, the student learns how to relate to a greater whole. This includes concrete technical aspects such as following tempo, matching dynamics and intonation, timing, etc., but also other consider-ations, for example cultivating a responsible attitude towards other group mem-bers, keeping appointments, attending rehearsals, being punctual, etc. In addition, all students participate in large-choir projects (Recently this included a perfor-mance of Bach's St. Matthew Passion and Carmina Burana, by Carl Orff.).

General cultural-historical knowledge is approached through studies of mu-sic history and analysis. Also, students specializing in music therapy can take 'In-troduction to composition and song-writing'. Here individuals can confront their practical experience and theoretical knowledge with their personal creative vision.

The musical training focuses on musical and clinical improvisation as the stu-dent delves into important frameworks such as tonal, modal and atonal harmony. Given a melodic or rhythmic motif, students will explore in-depth such techniques as mirroring, "containing" and pulsation. The development of improvisation skills takes place weekly during ample contact hours with faculty in both individual and various group settings. Students will also hone their skills by participating in gen-eral class projects as well as seminars and events led by improvisation experts from Europe and the USA.

6. Experiential learning, music therapy self experience

120 hours of group music therapy and 60 hours individual psychotherapy.

A student has to experience the training himself and therefore music therapy or psychotherapeutic self-experience is required. We expect the candidate music ther-apist to have a willingness to work alone, through a personal engagement in the training. This includes experiencing their own therapy, something that also holds true for the programme's lecturers and professors. This is because students can sense whether lecturers base their talks on their own therapeutic experiences or whether they have gone through a therapeutic process themselves. Without hav-ing experienced their own therapeutic process, they cannot adequately pass on the therapeutic phenomena and methods to their students; the professor's experience is as important as the textbook knowledge. For this, music therapists should grow with their own personal therapeutic experiences. There are many reasons for this, of which transference is among the most significant. Transference is one of the most important phenomena in a therapeutic relationship and students need to ex-perience this.

Once per week, music therapy students attend a two-hour music therapy group ses-sion. Self-experience in improvisation and self-reflection in a music therapeutic con-text is the main goal of this group. The group (maximum 8 students) begins meeting from the third year Bachelor and ends after two years. It is a closed group. The music therapist is independent and does not belong to the staff of the training course. The experiential group takes place in a different environment than the student's study en-vironment. By virtue of this, we hope to offer the students a very particular kind of therapeutic space where they can develop in both personal and interpersonal ways. By participating in musical improvisations and sharing verbal reflections afterwards, students can experience some musical group dynamics and group process. They experience the importance of the strongly protected framework of time and space, and they live the importance of shared professional confidentiality. During the two years of the experiential group, students first live and then symbolise personal and group dynamics in musical improvisation. This is the other important aim of this group: to foster awareness in both the individual and the group as a whole. This can engender feelings of love, acceptance and understanding. But it can also be the place of strong feelings such as rivalry, envy, frustration, contempt and misunderstanding. Witnessing empathic understanding as well as experiencing difficulties and how they may or may not be resolved can greatly enhance participant's personal growth as further music therapists.

7. Evaluation procedures concerning quality of teaching

The training programme is recognised from the government and was accredited by the VLUHR[3] in 2015. The accreditation was for the whole structure of LUCA, campus Lemmens (instrument/voice, jazz, composition, conducting, music education and music therapy). The music therapy programme was mentioned as excellent by the accreditation commission.

It is noteworthy that the music therapists and psychotherapists lecturing at our training facility are professors who maintain active positions in psychiatric hospitals or centres for handicapped people. It is important for the professors to refine their personal music therapy expertise, but also that they keep abreast with contemporary insights from in the increasingly active music therapy field.

8. PhD programme in music therapy

LUCA - Faculty of the Arts strives to be a European and global centre of excellence in artistic research. To this end, the research units focus on all areas of the arts practiced by students and teachers so that they develop into international artists and designers. By encouraging and developing PhDs in the arts, LUCA - Faculty of the Arts wants to attract young artistic researchers who help to reinforce and further develop its research and education. Given the need to build and bundle disciplinary expertise in all its study areas (music and drama, audio-visual arts, visual arts and design) LUCA - Faculty of the Arts fulfils an important role in attracting researchers, teachers and students with considerable talent and ambition. The research group Music Education & Therapy specializes in a practice-based approach with the aim at developing an "evidence-based" practice. The domain of music therapy includes the research in clinical and ambulatory child, adult and

---

3   VLUHR is authorized by the decree of 4th April, 2003, concerning the restructuring of higher education in Flanders (adjusted by the Education Decree XIX) to execute external quality assessments of educational programmes of Flemish universities, university colleges and other statutory registered institutions of higher education.

geriatric psychiatry, with a clear focus on effects of musical improvisation, musical and therapeutic processes, interventions in music therapy and specific therapeutic phenomena and their effects.

The research group co-operates with various KULeuven research groups, and is embedded in an international network such as the consortium for research and education of 8 universities: University of Melbourne, Aalborg University, Temple University, the University of Bergen, the University of Queensland, the University of Jyvaskyla, the Norwegian Academy of Music, Anglia Ruskin University and LUCA, School of Arts KULeuven.

The three main areas of collaboration are: International benchmarking in the evaluation of proposals, ethical procedures, and the supervision and examination of theses; Collaborative projects; and Research teaching and supervision.

LUCA regularly organises seminars for PhD students. The programme focuses on topics and methods specific to research in the arts. Doctoral students may also benefit from the programme offered by the Doctoral School for the Humanities and Social Sciences.

9. References

Bion, W.R. (1967). *Second Thoughts. Selected Papers on Psychoanalysis*. London: Maresfield Library.

De Backer, J., Foubert, K., & Van Camp, J. (2014). Lauschendes Spiel. Musiktherapeutische Interventionen in der Psychosenbehandlung ["Listening playing". Music therapeutic interventions in the treatment of psychosis]. *Die Psychodynamische Psychotherapie, 4*, 256-263.

De Backer, J., & Sutton, J., (Eds.). (2014). *The music in music therapy: Psychodynamic music therapy in Europe: Clinical, theoretical and research approaches*. London: Jessica Kingsley.

5   Aalborg, Denmark

Stine Lindahl Jacobsen and Lars Ole Bonde

©Rene Jeppesen, Musikkens Hus

©Courtesy of Department of Communication and Psychology, Aalborg University

Departement for Music Therapy
Aalborg University
http://www.musikterapi.aau.dk/musikterapiuddanelsen

Full time BA and MA Music Therapy Programme
Aalborg University, DNK

FACT SHEET

Institution:	Aalborg University, Denmark, Faculty of Humanities, Department of Communication and Psychology
	(The Program is located in "The House of Music" which is also home of Aalborg Symphony Orchestra, the Royal Academy of Music Aalborg and Musicology at Aalborg University)
Programme Head:	Ass. Prof. Dr. Stine Lindahl Jacobsen
Study Period:	6 semesters BA Music Therapy
	4 semesters MA Music Therapy
ECTS Credits:	120/180 (BA/MA)
Number of students:	Max. 40 (groups of 12/13 for BA; max. 15 for MA)
Teaching personnel:	2 Professors (2 x 1 FTE); 5 Associate professors (4 x 1 FTE, 1 x 0.75 FTF), 1 Assistant Professor (1 FTF), Secretary (0.75 FTE), PhD Students & Lecturers
Tuition Fee:	None
Target Group:	High school graduates and other relevant BAs such as music teachers in primary school, music pedagogues, musicians, nurses, psychologists, social workers
Adm. Requirements:	High school diploma or equivalent education (BA) with the necessary musical competencies to pass the entrance test. For MA-programme, BA in Music Therapy or equivalent education. There is an entrance test for both programmes
Language of Instr. :	Danish and English
Type:	Full-time Programme with Bachelor or Masters Degree
Academic Degree:	Bachelor and Master of Music Therapy (BA/MA)
Occupational Title:	Music Therapist
Others:	PhD Programme (see p. 70)

1. Background: Developments, theories, and philosophy

The programme in Aalborg embraces the current "multi-paradigm situation" of the discipline as it openly acknowledges the range of different scientific traditions which have influenced and still influences the reality of the profession. Each of these traditions has important theoretical, clinical and research-based contributions to the development of music therapy as a field. (Bonde, 2014; Wigram et al., 2001).

Fundamentally the Aalborg programme builds on a humanistic view on the idea of the human being and on music (Bonde, 2009; Ruud, 2010). The psychodynamic tradition still has an important role not only considered useful as a theoretical pre-understanding of the problems of clients but also as a basis for the development of the identity of the therapist. A humanistic view on the human being includes understanding it as a unity of body, mind and spirit which provides three levels and three perspectives on life common for everyone. Human beings are furthermore always located in a social and cultural context which must be considered. This view on the human being relates to an understanding of treatment where self-healing resources and strengths are acknowledged as inborn in every human being, and therapy must build on this and stimulate these inborn traits. Health and illness is not a question of either/or, and this problematic dichotomy is replaced by salutogenic thinking (Antonovsky, 1987). The teaching at the Aalborg programme relates to the health psychological perspective that health involves body, mind and spirit in a complex interaction. Health is best understood as a continuum that everyone is placed within depending on how she or he relates to and copes with the many crises, threats and stressors of life.

A humanistic view on music consider music as a manmade, cultural and socially routed way to self-expression, communication and interpersonal exchange. Music is a consciousness phenomenon (Bonny, 2002), where meaning is formed in creation of music (composition, improvisation, songwriting) and in the process of listening (in interaction with other persons, during active music listening). These two processes of meaning production are not identical, as music is always ambiguous, unable to express precise, denotative meaning like language. This is not considered a limitation, but a specific property of music that makes it an invaluable therapeutic tool. A humanistic understanding of music acknowledges that musical meaning is produced in a process and a context where the prerequisites, preferences and openness of the participants play an important role (Bonde, 2009).

Problem-based learning (PBL) with student project is one of the main pillars of Aalborg University. PBL is a well-known and acknowledged learning model. Basically it aims to learn through asking questions and wondering about a problem or challenge in the actual world. It is central that the student takes responsibility for his or her own learning and is able to reflect and problematize. This is not only practiced through the many projects and reports but also reveals itself in the way teachers view themselves as facilitators of learning. Teachers are not only professionals who convey complete knowledge but to collaborate with the student to find the best way to obtain knowledge, skills and competences. This on a level where the students do not learn by heart but gain the ability to apply and adapt knowledge, solve problems and critically reflect on choice of method and results.

The Aalborg programme is based on a belief system where the student must relate their own knowledge to the knowledge of others on many levels – for instance on how their view on man, music and recollection and method affects new knowledge and new theories and then again how this affect therapist-identity and everyday clinical practice. It is a constant spiraling movement between ontology, epistemology and methodology. The goal is for the student to integrate theory and practice with constant droplets of wonder, reflection and positioning throughout their entire education.

Theoretical knowledge and analytical reflection are central parts of the skills and competences of the academically educated music therapist. Music therapy has developed into a form of evidence-based treatment in many different clinical contexts from somatic and psychiatric hospitals, training and rehabilitation centers, nursing homes, hospices, and social institutions to activities in the community where different vulnerable groups experience inclusion, empowering and mastering through music. It is the aim of the music therapy training programme at Aalborg University to provide the students with sufficient knowledge of these problems and of different types of scientific thinking, theory building and practical research (paradigms). The training should make the students able to establish a positive dialogue with colleagues from other professions, based on an understanding of their view on human nature, on health and disease, on therapy and treatment. The theoretical and analytical tracks of the training provide the students with the basic knowledge and stimulate them to work independently and critically with topics relevant for clinical practice (Bonde, 2014). Each semester has its specific theoretical topic or frame:

- Music psychology
- Observation and description of clinical practice
- Developmental and neuropsychology
- Music therapy theory related to physical and psychological developmental challenges
- Music therapy theory related to somatic illnesses and somatic challenges
- Music therapy theory related to psychiatry and psychosocial challenges
- Theory of science and research methods

2. Admission criteria and admission procedures

Admission requirements:

Generally, all applicants for a Danish humanities undergraduate program must have completed a high school education. In addition for the music therapy programme, all applicants must write a motivation letter and pass an entrance test. The applicant must have some basic musical skills and these might not be apparent from a high school diploma. The audition is designed to test the applicant's skills in areas that are important for the implementation of music therapy training – and thus potential skills as a graduated music therapist.

During the 50 minutes audition the applicant must demonstrate basic skills in the main instrument (which can also be singing / voice), accompaniment instrument, voice and ear training. In addition, the applicant must demonstrate the ability to improvise, where the main instrument must be played by the student in an improvisational dialogue with one of the regular teaching staff. As music therapists often work with people with a limited expression potential, it is extremely important to have a good ear. Therefore, the audition includes ensuring that the applicant can remember and reproduce melodic phrases or rhythmic figures and can capture musical nuances in musical dialogues. The student must participate actively in three internships during the 10 semesters which is also why the audition includes an interview with focus on the applicant's own experiences (including therapy experience), motivation, maturity and self-insight.

3. Structure and content of the curriculum

In the first three years of the BA-programme all the basic skills must be developed, while the 2-year master programme qualifies the student to become a clinical music therapist with treatment responsibility. To ensure the graduated music therapist has the necessary skills to perform treatment with client groups with very different needs, the programme has three parallel tracks: music, theory, and therapy. In the beginning the three tracks are relatively separated, but gradually they are more integrated as the MA-programme primarily focuses on testing and reinforcing skills in relation to clinical practice.

Overview of the Structure of the Programme

Both BA- and MA-programme are fulltime. The semesters start in September and February with teaching until December and May. In June, August, and January the students take exams and do self-study work.

Course Contents

The 5-year MA programme provides profound competences within the following three 'tracks':

- Musical and improvisational knowledge & skills
- Theoretical and academic knowledge & skills
- Therapeutic knowledge & skills (self-experience as client and therapist) &
- Clinical practice (internship) and supervision

Competences mainly consist of following five areas:

1. To conduct clinical music therapy and assume treatment responsibility, including applying music therapy theory and empirical research to identify relevant music therapeutic strategies in relation to different client target groups
2. To use musical and music therapy techniques and skills to perform music activities and ensemble playing, to lead music listening groups and to conduct active and receptive music therapy processes for individuals and groups
3. To adopt an independent, professional and research-based approach to the study, analysis, documentation and processing of complex clinical issues, including planning, preparing and evaluating projects and reports
4. To take part in professional and interprofessional collaborations in accordance with current ethical guidelines music therapy targeted towards the needs of specific client target groups as regards the institutional and organisational contexts in which the music therapy takes place
5. To convert insight into own resources and developmental potential into clinical practice and to conduct music therapy treatment in accordance with ethical guidelines and under clinical supervision

Here is an overview of the modules of the Bachelor's and Master's Programme (Curriculum 2014).

Level	Name	ECTS
BA	Problem Based Learning	5
BA	Music Psychology	10
BA	Applied Musical Performance	10
BA	Training Therapy: Group Therapy 1-3	15
BA	Observation and Description of Clinical Practice	15
BA	Music Instruction 1+2	20
BA	Developmental Psychology and Neuropsychology	10
BA	Voice Work	10
BA	Improvisation	5
BA	Clinical Group Music Therapy Skills 1+2	15
BA	Clinical Body and Voice Work	5
BA	Group Supervision of Clinical Music Therapy	5

Level	Name	ECTS
BA	Songwriting in Music Therapy	5
BA	Music and Identity	5
BA	Theory of Music Therapy and Research 1-3 (including BA-thesis)	45
MA	Advanced Music Therapy Theory and Therapy Theory	10
MA	Clinical Improvisation 1+2	10
MA	Training Therapy: Individual Therapy	5
MA	Therapeutic, Psychodynamic Group Music Leading	5
MA	Advanced Music Therapy Theory and Research	15
MA	Inter Music Therapy	5
MA	Clinical Supervision, Individually and in Group	15
MA	Presentation and Communication of Clinical Music Therapy	15
MA	Music Therapy Assessment	5
MA	Guided Imagery and Music (level 1)	5
MA	Master's Thesis	30
	SUM	300

4. Clinical training, internships

As part of the programme the student has three internship periods – in the beginning and end of the Bachelor Programme and one full semester in the Master Programme. The student must follow a clinically working music therapist in a 4 weeks observational internship period in the second semester. All professional functions such as meetings with colleagues, conversations with relatives, writing reports, etc. are relevant for the students to follow as the aim is gain full insight into the music therapy practice in order to target the student's musical, therapeutic and theoretical knowledge and skills in the following semesters.

In the 6th semester the student enter internship again with one day a week for 10 weeks as a clinically working music therapist. The student receives clinical supervision to meet ethical standards and to ensure maximum learning outcome for the student. The BA-thesis is usually based on experiences from the internship. A 16-week part-time internship takes place in the 9th semester including individual and group supervision. The students are here expected to engage in long-term client processes. The MA-thesis is usually also based on data or experiences from the internship which enables integration between clinical experience and theoretical knowledge (Bonde, 2014; Holck, 2010).

5. Musical training

A music therapist must be very flexible in his or her musical expression. The music therapist needs to develop the expertise to choose the appropriate procedure and a musical expression that is concordant with the client's needs and within the therapist's competence. This means that the therapist must have knowledge of a broad and varied musical repertoire – from classical music to jazz and rock, and to 'therapy music' – and that he/she must be able to improvise on all sorts of instruments. The therapist must be a good singer and instrumentalist and have developed skills in playing sheet music, harmonic accompaniment, playing by ear and in free improvisations on, for example, a scale, mode, motif, image, mood or other 'givens'.

Among the special training disciplines of the Aalborg programme improvisational skills is essential (Wigram, 2004). The students learn how to let go of notes and improvise by means of focusing on musical parameters, moods, flexibility and variation. The training programme in Aalborg attaches great importance to improvisation, and improvisation skills are taught in order to qualify the students to use these skills in clinical practice with individual clients or groups. However, it is not enough just to develop good musical skills in singing, instrumental play and improvisation. The two cornerstones of the training are the development of the musical identity and the therapeutic identity and learning how to balance them.

Our ability to understand our clients through their music depends on our own musical sensitivity, skill and experience. Attaching meaning to clients' musical material is achieved by:

- being able to listen to their music
- being able to remember and/or notate their music
- being able to analyze their music
- being able to contextualize their music
- being able to interpret the meaning within their music. (Wigram, 2004)

At Aalborg University the students build a repertoire on their main instrument, and they learn to analyze music and to describe musical material with the use of musical terminology. They work intensely with improvisation skills, as they need to learn to replicate and match clients' musical themes, style of play vocally and instrumentally and also be able to describe their own approach and responses. Focus is especially on how the client or the therapist's music changes over time – within an improvisation or an entire session. Transitions represent change – in both the music itself and the client's pathological condition or common state. Being able to develop these transitions musically is an important music therapy skill and it is a musical skills.

The students prepare a "musical autobiography" built on their own memories and experiences. They describe and reflect on their musical background and musical development. From these autobiographies it is clear that the student's relationship with the main instrument is a lifelong process of development, with defeats and victories, and that the encounter with improvisation is a great and exciting challenge that pushes boundaries and contribute significantly to the development of a professional music therapeutic identity (Bonde, 2013).

During the course of the programme it is frequently discussed how directive or non-directive a music therapist should be. A more directive and structure oriented therapist's approach can be understood negatively as "manipulative" or "dominant". One can also perceive a therapist using advanced skills to frame a client's very simple music as directive, but this therapist's style can just as well be seen as supportive, "holding", inspiring and creative. The skills that students acquire should be at such a high level that he or she easily and with flow can find the right balance between following and taking initiative, between symbiosis and independence, between musical freedom and musical structure.

It is all about the balance between these elements: The combination of a variety of parts to a whole, which reaches the client. These elements and parts can be planned in advance, and they can occur intuitively derived or reactive but first and foremost, they must be sensitive and flexible (Bonde 2014; Wigram, 2004).

6. Experiential learning, music therapy self-experience

The Master programme trains therapeutic skills in the form of mandatory self-experience music therapy courses, therapeutic methodology courses and supervision. During the programme the students work psychotherapeutically on their own development building their music therapist identity and gradually gaining competence to work therapeutically and ethically responsible in their later professional life.

The therapeutic dimension track is divided into three different teaching methods. (1) Music therapy self-experience deals with personal and therapeutic development and integrates work with the student as client over time. The focus of work is to prepare for a future professional integrated and experienced identity as a music therapist (Lindvang, 2013; Lindvang & Bonde, 2012). (2) Therapeutic methodology courses deals with students alternating between being therapist and being client in order to develop learned methodological awareness. The focus is for the student to experience the different methods and approaches on his or her own body and mind in a setting where their own development and group dynamics can be made aware within individual sessions and short-term courses (Pedersen, 2002a, 2002b; Wigram, De Backer & Van Camp, 1999). Another important focus of this training is to increase knowledge of the possibilities and limitations of clinical methods and techniques in relation to different target groups. (3) Internships and supervision integrate the two first and expand the educational field in working with a specific client group and in functioning in a particular institutional context in order to develop an experienced professional identity.

Self-experience courses include:

• Group Therapy
• Individual music therapy
• Clinical Body and Voice Work

Self-experience modules are characterized as processes occurring over time. In all modules there is the opportunity to work with biographical themes, blockages, and anxieties perceived to be an obstacle to self-expression. The main purpose of self-experience therapy course is to give students the ability to manage the music therapist role and act with a natural authority in their future work. Thus, there will be work focused on themes that are basic to all therapists.

Therapeutic methodology:

• Clinical group music therapy skills
• Psychodynamic group management
• Inter Therapy
• Guided Imagery and Music (GIM), level 1

These courses are characterized by students learning by being a therapist and by entering into a client role for fellow students under the direct supervision of an experienced music therapist, and through extensive feedback processes with contributions from an experienced music therapist and from fellow students.

Supervision include:

• Internships and preparation
• Individual supervision
• Group Supervision

Both self-experience therapy and therapeutic methodology course serve as a preparation for making optimal use of both individual and group supervision in connection with internships and in connection with future professional practice. The focus here is related to the supervisee's current work situation.

7. Evaluation procedures concerning quality of teaching

The Aalborg Programme has existed for over 30 years and is a fixed part of the quality assurance of Aalborg University including ongoing and systematic evaluation and development of new university educations. This involves annual fixed term evaluations of teaching, educations, curriculum, etc. for the Board of Studies for music therapy. Evaluation work is done in dialogue with the board of external examiners, Faculty of Humanities, Department of Communication and Psychology and the advisory board and provides the basis for the Board of Studies' action plan for further development of education.

In 2012 the Board launched a special training programme, called "Applied music in social, educational and health care settings" (Danish acronym: PROMUSA), in Copenhagen. (60 ECTS, two year part time). This training is open for applicants with BA diplomas in relevant interdisciplinary areas – such as music teachers, psychologists, social workers, musicians, etc. who also have the sufficient musical skills to pass the entrance test. The mix of different educational backgrounds ensures interdisciplinary collaboration and understanding. After finishing PROMUSA, the students can continue in the MA program if they pass the entrance test.

The Board of Studies is conscious about its responsibility to listen to and act on external and internal critique and to adapt and adjust the curriculum in order to always increase the quality of teaching and developed skills of the students. The students of the music therapy programme are engaged and motivated and evaluations show a general satisfaction among the students, who also tend to be very involved in the programme.

8. PhD Programme

The doctoral programme in music therapy at Aalborg University was established in 1996. Over 40 theses have successfully been submitted and defended at a public viva. The programme is closely connected with the teaching and research milieu at the MA programme in music therapy. With a majority of international scholarship students, the programme has a strong global orientation and partnership with front research milieus. International liaisons are fostered through well-established consortium partnerships, research networks and proficient data collection sites.

The goal of the doctoral programme is to train researchers with sufficient theoretical, technical, methodological and applied clinical research knowledge in the field of music therapy research to assure scientific rigor. The 30 ECTS biannual courses includes a rich mixture of course work and aim to cover the following topics of learning: a) Reflexive methodology including data administration and data analysis, b) Objectivistic methodology including data administration and statistical analysis, c) Research ethics and reflexivity, d) Theory of science, and e) Academic writing and dissemination (Wigram, 2008).

9. References

Antonovsky, A. (1987). *Unraveling the mystery of health: How people manage stress and stay well*. San Francisco, CA: Jossey-Bass.

Bonde, L.O. (2009). *Musik og Menneske, Introduktion til musikpsykologi* [Music & human. Introduction to musicology]. Frederiksberg: Samfundslitteratur.

Bonde, L.O. (2013). The musical identities of Danish music therapy students: A study based on musical autobiographies. In Bonde, L.O., Ruud, E., Skånland, M., & Trondalen, G. (Eds.), *Musical Lifestories – health musicking in everyday life. Skriftserie fra Senter for musikk og helse* (Vol. 6, pp. 307-328). Oslo: NMH-Publikationer.

Bonde, L.O. (2014). *Musikterapi – Teori, Uddannelse, Praksis, Forskning* [Music therapy – Theory, training, practice, research]. Aarhus: Forlaget Klim.

Bonny, H. (2002). *Music and Consciousness: The Evolution on guided Imagery and Music.* (Ed. L. Summer). Gilsum NH: Barcelona Publishers.

Holck, U. (2010). Supervision af novicemusikterapeuter i arbejde med børn med betydelige og varige funktionsnedsættelser [Supervision of novice music therapists with in the field of children with delvelopmental disorder]. In K. Stensæth, A.T. Eggen, & R.S. Frisk (Eds.), *Musikk, helse, multifunksjonshemming. Skriftserie fra Senter for musikk og helse* (Vol. 2, pp. 89-104). Oslo: NMH-Publikationer.

Lindvang, C. (2013). Resonant learning: a qualitative inquiry into music therapy students' self-experiential learning processes. *Qualitative Inquiries in Music Therapy 8*, 1-30. Gilsum: Barcelona Publishers. Open access via http://www.barcelonapublishers.com/resources/QIMTV8/QIMT8-1_Lindvang.pdf

Lindvang, C., & Bonde, L.O. (2012). Følelser i bevægelse. Om læreprocesser i musikterapeutens uddannelse [Emotion in motion. About learning processes in the music therapist education]. *Psyke & Logos, 33*(1), 87-116.

Pedersen, I.N. (2002a). Self-Experience for music therapy students. Experiential training in music Therapy as a methodology: A mandatory part of the music therapy programme at Aalborg University. In J. Th. Eschen (Ed.), *Analytical Music Therapy* (pp. 168-190). London: Jessica Kingsley.

Pedersen, I.N. (2002b). Psychodynamic Movement: A basic training methodology for music therapists. In J. Th. Eschen (Ed.), *Analytical Music Therapy* (pp. 190-216). London: Jessica Kingsley.

Ruud, E. (2010). *Music therapy: a perspective from the humanities.* Gilsum, NH: Barcelona Publishers.

Wigram, T. (2004). *Improvisation. Methods and techniques for music therapy clinicians, educators and students.* London: Jessica Kingsley.

Wigram, T. (2008). Doctoral research school in music therapy, Aalborg University. Muziek Therapie Nieuwsbrief. *Muziek, 21*, 12-17.

Wigram, T., De Backer, J., & Van Camp, J. (1999). Music therapy training: a process to develop the musical and therapeutic identity of the music therapist. In T. Wigram, & J. De Backer (Eds), *Clinical applications of music therapy in developmental disability, paediatrics and neurology* (pp. 201-223). London: Jessica Kingsley.

Wigram, T., Nygaard-Pedersen, I., & Bonde, L. O. (Eds.). (2001) *A Comprehensive Guide to Music Therapy. Theory, Clinical Practice, Research and Training.* London: Jessica Kingsley.

6   Paris, France

Edith Lecourt

©Edith Lecourt

©Edith Lecourt

MA Music Therapy Programme
University Sorbonne Paris City/ Paris Descartes and Sorbonne Nouvelle (SPC-P5/P3), Paris

http://odf.parisdescartes.fr/formations/feuilleter-le-catalogue/sciences-humaines-et-sociales-SHS/master-lmd-XB/master-creation-artistique-specialite-musicotherapie-program-amf45-421-html

Full time Two-Year MA Music Therapy Programme

University Sorbonne Paris City/Paris Descartes and Sorbonne Nouvelle

FACT SHEET

Institution:	Organized by two Universities: Paris 5/Paris Descartes and Paris 3/Sorbonne Nouvelle
Programme Heads:	Prof. Todd Lubart with Associate Professor Mireille Naturel
Study Period:	4 semesters (M1 = first year, M2 = second year)
ECTS Credits:	120
Number of students:	20 per year
Teaching personnel capacities:	Director and Assistant Director (0.5 FTE), Secretary (0.75 FTE), Administration (0.3 FTE), Teachers: about 8 full professors, 6 associate professors, 10 music therapists (all part-time)
Tuition Fees:	Students: None (except approx. 300 € for annual inscription) Professionals (cont. education): about 12,667 € (in total)
Target Group:	Students; some places for professionals
Adm. Requirements:	Motivation letter with documents, interview with the responsible persons. Required are: License Degree (in particular, psychology, musicology, educational sciences, social sciences, medicine), current musical practice, previous experience in social or educational or health work. For entering directly to M2: plus Diploma equivalent of Music Therapy.
Language of Instr.:	French
Type:	Full time Programme with Master's Degree
Academic Degree:	LMD European Degree = Master Professional and Research in Music Therapy
Occupational Title:	Sorbonne Paris City Master of Human and Social Sciences, mention Artistic Creation, specialization Music therapy
Others:	LMD European Degree: Doctorate of Arts Therapies (three years). The Doctorate School ED456/566 is a composition of 3 Universities with main orientations on body, movement (dance) and handicaps.

Université Sorbonne Paris Cité/Paris Descartes - UFR STAPS - 1 rue Lacretelle - 75015 Paris. Contact: Secrétariat: scolarite.master@staps.parisdescartes.fr

1. Background: Developments, theories, and philosophy

Since 1972 many training programmes in music therapy have been developed in France, through associations and, since the eighties also through some universities "D.U." diplomas for specializations (mainly for health or educational professionals). These diplomas are free (not depending on universities criteria). They are not integrated in the LMD European programme (LMD = Licence – Master – Doctorat).

It is why we created a Master programme in 2011 and a Doctorate in 2013. The Master specialization music therapy is one of the four masters of arts therapies included in our programme (together with dance therapy, plastic arts therapy, drama therapy). These masters are supported by two universities: Paris 5/ Paris Descartes and Paris 3/Sorbonne Nouvelle. As a consequence these masters are on a "meta level" of the French university organization: Sorbonne Paris City in which are eight universities and institutes associated. On this institutional point of view I feel this "meta level" essential for the existence and survival of these trainings. With these master and doctorate, the specialization of music therapy, as the others specializations, is now included in the LMD European programme.

This master is the result of more than fourty years of teaching music therapy in France at different levels. This history is at its foundation (and influences the three other masters of arts therapies). A "temptation" of behavioral orientation (with commercial facilities) was identified during the beginning of the seventies and was at the origin of a counter orientation through the psychoanalytic French development in psychology and psychiatry. These last specialties: psychology, psychoanalysis, psychopathology and psychiatry were the main domains offering theoretical background for a clinical music therapy. The first development of music therapy in France was in hospitals and especially in psychiatric departments (beginning 1801 Philippe Pinel who associated music for the recovery phases of psychiatric patients). But since the 1990s more and more demands were received from the social and educational domains and, as a consequence, offer a new background in social and educational sciences.

Three domains of applications are now well identified and developed with their different theories: social, educational, health (with still a big place for psychiatry).

Yet the courses give a general presentation of the different clinical theories (psychotherapies, social sciences and education), with an especial development on phenomenology and psychoanalysis (Freud, Winnicott, Klein, Jung, Lacan etc.) enlarged with group analysis and institutional analysis (the French theoretical school of group, family and institutional psychoanalysis with principal authors: Didier Anzieu, René Kaës, Jean-Claude Rouchy etc., but also Bion or Foulkes). On a research point of view we have also presentations of the neurocognitive researches on music (developed in France in two universities Caen and Dijon with Bigan and Lechevallier).

My own theory on music therapy is presented and practically experienced, as a fundament of their training (Analytic Group Music therapy, sonorous communication). It uses precisely the sound and music acoustics and a structural analysis of the way they are produced in a clinical relationship. It is a confrontation with the group psychoanalysis concepts ("group illusion", "group envelop", "basic assumptions" etc.) with the musical concepts. The group dimension (unconscious) of the psychic structure (individual or groupal) is in connection with the group structure of music, a polyphonic structure, opposite and complementary, to the verbal monody of the verbal language structure. The applications of this theory need a precise observation and analysis of the sonorous/musical production inside the relational process. This production is the center; it is the condensation of the relation through the art.

Different practical methods of music therapy are presented. The students are invited to find their own way. We teach them the necessity, deontological, to be clear in our personal orientation, our inside representations, our knowledge of the concepts, authors (as possible models), our theoretical and clinical choices. They have a teaching on deontology and ethics.

The students are also confronted with the theoretical development of the three others specialties of arts therapies, with different influences, for example on Maslow's humanistic theory.

Finally, they are invited to open their curiosity to the international level of music therapy (authors, methods, trainings) and to participate to the annual International Master Class of Arts Therapies organized by the Master.

2. Admission criteria, admission procedures

There are three criteria for admission: the "must have"

- Candidates must have already a License Degree (with preference to psychology, musicology, educational sciences, social sciences, medicine). The domain of the License is not obligatory.

- Candidates must have a current musical practice (a level enough to improvise), instrumental and/or vocal (a minimum of three years, generally more than five years)

- Candidates must have (with some exceptions possible) a previous experience in social or educational or health work (internships, animations… or professional experience)

If they have these criteria their candidature is examined.

There is a possibility to candidate directly for the M2 for candidates who have a diploma equivalent of Music Therapy from other schools or countries (equivalence for the M1). A commission examines separately these cases.

There is the possibility for the music therapists, professionals, who have some years of experience in music therapy to candidate to VAE (Validation of professional experience) and obtain part or totality of the M2, through a peculiar procedure.

Admission procedures:

The procedures are on internet only, through the web of the university; between April and June (to begin in September).

With their identities data they have to give the usual CV and a second CV: the artistic CV with their artistic cursus (in music and eventually others artistic activities).

They have to provide any justification of their License and others diplomas, work experiences etc.

These data are verified by the administration, and then given to the head of the specialty of music therapy who decides with the pedagogical commission which dossiers are relevant. These candidates are then invited for an interview.

The goal of the interview is to create a relationship and to try to find an answer to questions coming from the student's documents, to explore the candidate's relation to music (some come with musical productions, with program of concerts, musical activities they have done etc.) It is also to explain some points of the training and to answer the candidates' questions.

The issue of all the interviews of the candidates is a list of the candidates who are accepted.

These last candidates (the lucky ones!) are invited to proceed at their administrative and pedagogical registrations.

3. Structure and content of the curriculum

M1 and M2 are composed of 10 modules (UE: teaching unities), each one of 40 hours (part theory and part practice).

Some are common to the four specialties, others are peculiar and reserved to music therapists (about 50% in M1, and 70% in M2).

The training is organized with intensive week sessions (50 hours) of courses at the university which alternate with time for practices in institutions. There are about 8 such sessions/year. This is facilitation for students coming from different parts of France and from foreign countries.

M1: Semester 1:

UE 1, 2 and 4 give a common background for the four specialties

- UE 1: develops the "Fundaments on arts theories, history of arts and analysis" For example: a reflection on the ruptures in the arts developments (with specialists of dance, plastic arts, music and theater/drama)
- UE 2: develops the "basic theories and methodologies of the arts therapies". It has also to offer a first initiation in research in arts therapies with a preparation of a research dissertation (on a personal research) for the end of the year.
- UE 3: "Clinical practice and supervision in music therapy"; and professional identity, ethics and deontology. This is a work on their placements experiences: difficulties of the music therapist in institutions, presentation of situations, case analysis, relational art therapeutic difficulties etc. (through group exchanges, discussion, play, with a supervisor).
- UE 4: "Psychopathology and clinical practice in arts therapies": adult psychopathology and presentation of different applications of the arts therapies in the three domains: clinical, educative and social; case studies.
- UE 5: Experiential workshop 1. Different situations are played (role playing) and analyzed with the students. There is an initiation to the music therapy relationship with different clients, and to different methods of music therapy; Initiation to the "sonorous communication" in the group (development of self consciousness, of quality of listening and sonorous interaction).

M1: Semester 2:

UE 6 and 9 are common to the four specialties of arts therapies

- UE 6: "Places and functions of the body in the arts therapies"; this is a common reflection for all the students with teachers of the different specialties. This UE develops the concepts of perception, communication, through the different arts, with an introduction to the aesthetic emotion.
- UE 7: "Methodology, case study in music therapies and applications psycho/socio/cultural". From cases studies, development of knowledge in psychopathology, handicaps, and reflection on different practical situations.
- UE 8: Clinical practice, supervision, and research. This UE is a continuation of UE2 (research) and 3. It has to validate, at the end of the year, the clinical practice (practice placements) and the personal research of the student (research dissertation).
- UE 9: "The different publics and applications of the arts therapies (educative/social/health)", how to adapt the methodologies to the clients, at each age of life, and with different personal and social difficulties. Examples are given by different arts therapists.

- UE 10: This is an optional programme. The student is invited to build a personal programme with courses given in universities, conferences of congresses etc. with the goal to develop his/her competences and knowledge in music therapy. This is validated by the head of the music therapy programme and finally evaluated by an oral examination.

Assessment of the M1: written examinations on table, oral examination, evaluation of the experiential workshop, validation of the clinical work (in institutions) essays, and documentations. The research dissertation is presented to a jury.

M2 Semester 3:

UE 11 is common to the four specialties

The students are invited to develop their competencies on research with the choice of the research option (non obligatory). In this case they have research teaching and a new research dissertation to realize together with the professional development (obligatory).

- UE 11: "Art, aesthetic and therapy" this is a common reflection on the role of art and aesthetics in the arts therapies. Teachers from the different specialties develop this theme with the support of concepts like idealization, sublimation, defense mechanisms, with a reflection on the peculiar processes of a clinical relationship through the arts.
- UE 12: "Music therapy practices in education/social situations/clinical work" the students are invited to present cases studies (from their practical placements) and develop their capacities of analysis and of music therapeutic relationship. They are given more knowledge on pathologies and handicaps.
- UE 13: Clinical practice, supervision and professional identity (ethics and deontology). Work on the clinical situations encountered in their placements in a group of supervision.
- UE 14: Experiential workshop 2, experience and analysis. In the experiential situations proposed, the student is invited to initiate clinical settings and to animate some situations with the group. This work is supervised by music therapists.

  For example: The students have to be able to analyze a situation of group sonorous communication, through the acoustic registration of a session (acoustic, musical, and relational analysis).

- UE 15: Methodology: the student choose between

- **ECUE** research dissertation **and** professional dissertation

- **ECUE** professional dissertation

The students have seminars to help them for each dissertation, and a special full week programme on research with presentations of different researchers (from universities and the National Research Center) on problematic, methodology, evaluation, statistics etc.

M2 Semester 4

- UE 16: International practices and researches. The students are invited to search and realize a document on an international level. Music therapists who have been trained in other countries are invited to present their training and practices. This UE is developed through our annual International Master Class of Arts Therapies (in June/July). The students are also encouraged to participate to congresses out of France.

- UE 17: Fundaments of arts therapies practices. This is a complementation on theories, concepts, settings, methodologies of assessment, of observation, of case studies etc.

- UE 18: Clinical practice and research in arts therapies. Supervisions of clinical practices and realization of the professional dissertation.

- Supervisions of researches (for the student who have chosen this option) and realization of the research dissertation. The dissertations are finally presented to a jury.

- UE 19: Development and research. Development of anthropology, neuroscience, philosophical, psychological, and sociological aspects. Synthesis of professional competences and preparation of a professional project. The students who have chosen the research option present and discuss their research process in a "mini colloquium" with the participation of all the specialties.

- UE 20: Optional UE: The student is invited to create his own program with precise training goals. His/her program is composed by participations to universities complementary courses (In France or in other countries), congresses etc. His/her project is validated by the head of the specialty. The final examination is oral.

M2 Assessment:

Validation of the clinical practice (from placements institutions), participation in supervision and experiential situations, different documents, oral (UE 20), written examinations "on table" (less in M2 than in M1), collective presentation of their professional dissertation and professional project; and for the research option, presentation of the research dissertation to a jury.

4. Clinical training, internships

Total internships: 500h (M1 200 + M2 300)

The students are invited to search a place for their internships. Some indications are given from the experiences of the precedent students, but they have to find by themselves. They can find their internship either in health departments, in educational institutions, or in social institutions. They are invited to make diverse experiences through these two years (minimum 2 different places).

This clinical experience is supervised at the university (in group sessions cf. UE 3, 8, 13 and 18)

5. Musical training

There is no musical training in the Master. The students have their musical practice and learning at their own responsibility, as their personal musical development. They can be oriented, if necessary, by teachers of the Master.

6. Experiential learning, music therapy self experience

An experiential learning is organized in two parts of the programme and within the two years. Part of the experiential learning is in the common programme with the three others specializations of arts therapies and working about the body in the relation of art therapy, the movement, the image, the sound etc… all common questions in experiential situations, with the different specialist.

The other part is inside the specialization of music therapy, limited to this specialty with the goal to deepen the student's personal experience and to develop his/her capacities of observation and analysis. Other workshops are on the animation of a clinical situation with the group of student.

The development of group analysis and music therapy, in a group sonorous communication, is offered through successive sessions, to deepen the process, with the goal to give the student, through his/her own experience (new consciousness), a veritable clinical instrument.

The "Bilan psychomusical" is also the opportunity for self experience, in a group, and the learning of a clinical instrument for evaluation before and after music therapy sessions.

Sessions of receptive music therapy, and sessions of relaxation with music complete this personal introduction to the applications of music therapy.

More generally, the students of the four specialties of arts therapies are encouraged to develop their self-consciousness through psychotherapies, or psychoanalysis and/or arts therapies.

7. Evaluation procedures concerning quality of teaching

This evaluation is organized each year by the University for all the Masters (generally through questionnaires and statistics). During the years there are times for exchanges on the organization and contents of the training (generally at the end of a week session), with the teachers, the head of the specialty and the head of the four specialties.

8. PhD Programme

The PhD programme for the research doctorate training is organized by the Doctorate School which receives the Doctorate of Arts Therapies. It is a three years (4 maximum) programme with about 10 technical modules on how to develop research, statistics, article writing (for all the doctorates of different domains), and seminars on specialties. Each student is directed by two researchers habilitated for this responsibility.

The Doctorate School: ED456/566 is a composition of three Universities with main orientations on body, movement, handicaps. At the University Paris Descartes (one of the three), "TEC" is the name of the laboratory in which is developed the Doctorate of Arts Therapies.

Before the existence of this Doctorate, students have presented a doctorate research on music therapy in psychology, or musicology or educational sciences. They have now the possibility of a total university development to defend the profession.

9. References

Internet sources:

http://www.staps.parisdescartes.fr/FORMATIONS/Master
http://formations.parisdescartes.fr/fr-FR/1/diplome/P5-PROG12173/MASTER%20
     Sorbonne%20Paris%20Cit%C3%A9,%20mention%20Arts-th%C3%A9rapies:
     %20Musicoth%C3%A9rapie
Doctorate School: http://www.ed-456.u-psud.fr/ (Laboratory TEC)

7   Augsburg, Germany

Hans-Ulrich Schmidt and Tonius Timmermann

©Satzinger-Viel

©Courtesy of Leopold Mozart Centre

Department of Music Therapy
University of Augsburg, Leopold Mozart Centre
http://www.philso.uni-augsburg.de/en/lmz/Institute/Institute_of_Music_
Education_Music_Therapy_and_Musicology/Music_Therapy/

Part-time Postgraduate Music Therapy Programme
University of Augsburg, Leopold Mozart Centre, DEU

FACT SHEET

Institution:	University of Augsburg, Germany, The Leopold Mozart Centre for Music and Music Education
Programme Heads:	Prof. em. Dr. rer. biol. hum. Tonius Timmermann
	Prof. Dr. med. Hans Ulrich Schmidt
	Prof. Dr. sc. mus. habil. Susanne Metzner (starting in May 2016)
Study Period:	6 semesters
ECTS Credits:	120
Number of students:	Max. 14 per study group
Teaching personnel capacities:	C3-Professorship, W2- Professorship (0.5 FTE), Research Assistant (0.5 FTE), Secretary (0.5 FTE), Lectureships
Tuition Fee:	500 €/semester (exclusive personal experience supervision)
Target Group/ Addressees:	Professionals in suitable occupations (e.g. music pedagogues, doctors, psychologists, social workers)
Adm: Requirements:	BA- or an equivalent degree, 3 years of experience, clinical internship (4 weeks), self-experience (15 single, 15 group sessions), suitability test
Language of Instr.:	German
Type:	Part-time programme with Master's Degree
Academic Degree:	Master of Arts (M.A.)
Occupational Title:	Music Therapist
Others:	PhD Programme (see p. 92)

The following link provides further information: http://www.philso.uni-augsburg.de/en/lmz/Institute/Institute_of_Music_Education_Music_Therapy_and_Musicology/Music_Therapy/

1. Background: Developments, theories, and philosophy

Underlying is an idea of man, which holistically integrates the diversity of the sentiments of the mind and corresponding sounds, like they are expressed in music therapy. Consonance and dissonance are, thereby, part of the human personality, correspondent to the overtone series in music as analyzed by Pythagoras. Additionally, one should mention another Greek philosopher of the middle stoicism, Panaitios. He was not in favour of the passed down ethical demands for the generally binding personality ideals and said that one can only expect from a human that she or he fulfils their own ideal. In other words, to develop and act out the depth of the possibilities given to a human is a substantial thought that the fundamentals of modern, therapeutic ethics describe. Wilhelm von Humboldt pursued such approaches and applied them in the 18th century to the ideal of humanity in education as full development of the personality. These concepts are fundamental for the later "Declaration of Human Rights". Heidegger sets the possibility higher in contrast to the reality. With this, he philosophically opens the human's work to his developmental potential. *"Wahr-sein"* ["To be true"] has to be equivalent to *"entdeckend-sein"* ["being discovering"]; translated to depth psychological language it means: the human reaches his true self through working on uncovering himself (Timmermann, 2004, p. 48 ff).

If psychotherapy wants to do more than just eliminate symptoms, it has to deal with the historical development of consciousness and society in order to understand a modern individual that is seeking help. Alienation, loneliness, isolation, decline of relationships and social environments, or lacking experiences of authenticity are modern disease-causing phenomena. Winnicott's model and implementations of *"false"* and *"true"* *"self"* provide a good direction for the psychotherapeutic objectives (Winnicott, 1984). The *"self"* is thereby more than the *"I"*: It is a relationship form characterized by a connection of the *"I"* and the unconscious and conscious, the familiar, and the sociocultural overall whole. Self-realization can only happen in a relationship. It enables the development of the specific potential and profile of the individual and at the same time, enables the placement in a larger, overall whole. The supporting of experiences and consciousness is especially important in self-experience within the framework of an artistic and body-oriented approach.

Psychotherapy needs an ethical orientation that does not necessarily tie up with a specific religious or cultural tradition, but that is in harmony with human rights that define the modern codex for intercultural ethics and questions about the handling of patients. The full unfolding of personality belongs to the human dignity, which can be used as a guideline for therapeutic actions.

The Masters programme in Augsburg sees itself as training in music therapy that takes place in accordance with depth psychology. Thinking in depth psychology, or psychodynamically, is the basis of modern psychotherapeutic thought and action that is expanded through humanistic, systemic, and behavioural and/or polypragmatic approaches. In summary, we are taking an integrative, eclectic approach that

chooses therapeutic means and ways due to their specific indications and their necessity in a clinical setting and explore their effectiveness. As a guide, music therapists need a cartography of the soul and of mental processes. Traditional depth
psychological thinking is complemented by components of humanistic therapy
that focus on actions and the body and is expanded through systemic approaches
and also occasionally through behavioural approaches.

Music in music therapy is seen as a symbolic language that includes conscious
and unconscious symbolization. Language is thereby not necessarily a requirement for symbolization. On the contrary, language is based on the implicit ability
of the human to symbolize. Nonverbal psychotherapies use spontaneous symbolization. In music therapy, symbolization occurs on two levels: first on the level of
the instrument (choice of instrument, way of playing) and second on the level of
the musical dynamic. Musical symbolization is used both diagnostically and therapeutically (Schmidt & Timmermann, 2012).

2. Admission criteria and admission procedures

Admission requirements:

- Completed musical, medical, psychological, pedagogical or an equivalent degree
- Three years of professional experience or activity in a relevant working field
- Personal experience: Minimum of 15 hours single and group music therapy each
- Clinical internship, if possible in an area relevant for music therapy or an
  equivalent activity. This can be done as a four-week internship or over a longer period of time with 1-2 intern days a week. A total of 100 hours should be
  completed, of which a third should be therapy shadowing.

- Passing of a four-part suitability test
  1. Music theory: Notes and rhythm dictation in the difficulty level of a folk-
     song; fluent playing of cadences and minor parallels in all keys, and harmo-
     nization of a simple folksong on the piano
  2. Instrument and Vocal Testing:
  – Prelude of two pieces of moderate difficulty from different eras/styles on the
     main instrument; Piano: Two pieces in at least the difficulty level of a sonatina,
     a simple sonata, or an invention of Bach in two voices. If piano is the main in-
     strument, easier pieces should be performed on a second instrument.
  – Vocal or instrumental performance of a piece from a style of choice. (Dem-
     onstration of the own musical sense)
  – Vocal testing: Performance of two songs with own accompaniment;
  3. Improvisation: Spontaneous musical assignment, alone and in a group
  4. Individual interview about the motivation of the applicant

Explanations:

The curricular circumstances of the concept of a part-time Masters programme for which the students have already earned a previous degree and at least three years of experience in a suitable profession, are justified by:

- Life and professional experience of the participants

- The application of music therapeutic competence into related or suitable fields

- Possible occupational change to a primarily music therapeutic job

- Trans-regional distribution of internships and training therapy (by having students organise these themselves, e.g. close to their homes)

The different artistic and scientific experiences of the members of the heterogeneous group are integrated into the course of studies. These complement each other and at the same time allow for specialisations. Self-experience and an internship are supposed to help the candidates verify their own motivation through self-reflection in a therapeutic setting and the encounter of clinical situations.

The musical part of the admissions test determines whether the applicant fulfils the requirements for the musical training in the Masters programme. Musicality and an identity as a musician or as someone who makes music are necessary. One should have a special relationship with two or more instruments, of which one would ideally be the piano. It is not musical excellence that is relevant, but the openness to improvised playing of several instruments and to various music styles in the way they are encountered by the music therapist in previous experiences and by the preferences of patients. Not only is the mentioned musicality tested, but also how far the candidate is willing to apply it to situations with patients. Basically, it is determined whether a candidate shows enough potential to reach the musical goals of the education as described in the curriculum.

Students whose native language is not German must provide evidence of the required proficiency in the language of instruction. The audit committee will decide on individual cases.

3. Structure and content of the curriculum

The further training one receives through this programme, which complies with all modern standards, is thought to allow application of music therapeutic competence into appropriate fields, but also serves as a qualification to introduce music therapy work in new, potentially suitable institutions. Our programme follows the standard of the DMtG within the certifications.

Moreover, further emphases are laid on the scientific qualifications of graduates in order to further establish quality management in music therapy through primary, application-oriented research. The Masters programme is strongly linked to our research unit "music and health" and their activities.

Overview of the structure of the programme

The programme is designed to be a three-year (6 semester), part-time, postgraduate programme, that takes place in four weekend blocks (Thursday to Sunday) and two long blocks that include the weekend (9 days) per semester. The total of 1080 group class sessions are spread over the years:

- 24 Weekend blocks (1 block with max. 30 units, 24 blocks with max. 720 units)
- 6 Long blocks for 9 days (1 block with max. 72-90 units, 6 blocks with max. 390-540 units)

Additionally, there are events that students are expected to organise themselves:

- A two-part clinical internship   210
- Individual music therapy self-experience   100
- External, individual supervision   30
- Prior to commencement of studies
  - 4 week long internship
  - 15 hours individual self-experience
  - 15 hours group self-experience

Course contents

As can be seen in a later overview of the modules and module parts, the programme provides profound knowledge and skills in every artistic and scientific area being of significance for the future music therapist:

- Basic-knowledge of music therapy relevant music anthropological, scientific, and psychological topics
- Training in music practical skills for clinical work
- Knowledge and practice of the active and receptive music therapy approaches
- Fundamental knowledge in various theoretical and methodological approaches that are used internationally
- Practicing of conversational skills as well as adequate, verbal attunement to the nonverbal music therapy activities and their subsequent processing
- State of the art in research and research methods in music therapy and music medicine
- Clinical music therapy training in typical music therapy areas
- Medical, psychological, psychotherapeutic basic and specialised knowledge
- Self-reflective skills alone and in groups

The training concept as a whole therefore integrates the following elements:

- Artistic and psychological self-experience
- Specific instrumental and vocal development
- Role-play and rehearsing in the group
- Insight in the practical work, its documentation, reflection, and research
- Music therapy research and relevant research from neighbouring disciplines

Here is an overview of our 14 modules for orientation. A more detailed version can be found on our homepage (www.leopold-mozart-zentrum.de):

		CH	VN	WL	CP
M1	Theoretical, scientific fundamentals	120	240	360	12
M2	Fundamental Music Skills	90	150	240	8
M3	Music Therapy Praxeology	90	180	270	9
M4	Self-reflective Skills I	110	40	150	5
M5	Foundations of Medicine	50	100	150	5
M6	Expertise of Medicine I	100	200	300	10
M7	Foundations of Psychotherapy	50	100	150	5
M8	Special Music Therapy Theory and Research	90	80	270	9
M9	Specific Music Skills	60	90	150	5
M10	Clinical Music Therapy	180	---	540	18
M11	Self-reflective Skills II	110	40	150	5
M12	Expertise of Medicine II	60	120	180	6
M13	Specific Psychotherapy Expertise	70	140	210	7
M14	Master's thesis und Presentation	---	---	480	16
	TOTAL	120 CP			

(CH (contact hours): events to complete; VN: expected time for preparation and follow-up; WL (workload): total workload; CP (credit points): total credit points)

4. Clinical training, internships

The students receive lessons in four different clinics in Augsburg (Psychiatry, Child and Adolescent Psychiatry, Paediatrics, Geriatrics) from doctors working in music therapy relevant areas. They will not only receive a theoretical introduction into the respective medical field, but also an insight into inpatient processes including ward rounds and case presentations.

The internships usually take place in a time period between the third and sixth semester. One of the internships should be done with children or adolescents, and one with adults. One of the two internships should be inpatient.

The internships include 250 hours in total, which are structured as:

- 50 hours of work shadowing and reflection with the internship instructor, participating in team meetings
- 100 hours of work with patients (alone and in groups)
- 30 hours of external single supervision
- 70 hours of preparation, reworking, and documentation

The internships are documented in an internship report. Internship preparation and support are not only supported from the respective instructor, but also from two mandatory courses ("Internship Preparation Seminar", "Seminar for Support During Internship") that are held by the heads of this programme. This is done in order to convey the music therapy and also the medical perspective. At the same time, suggestions and ideas for (usually application-oriented) Masters' theses will be discussed and reflected upon.

5. Musical training

The content of the musical training is based on fundamental music therapy approaches (Timmermann, 2014). This is valid for both the practical and the theoretical competences. In order to accomplish the musical techniques within the music therapy situations, it is necessary to complete a specific training that includes exercises at home. Requirements are musicality, identity as a musician, openness to improvisation, as well as specific musical skills, which are tested in advance (see above, section 2: Admission criteria and admission procedures). Especially considering the relationship oriented psychotherapeutic aspects, special attention should be given to voice and rhythm in our opinion.

The musical competences that are to be acquired, primarily follow the repertoire of active and receptive music therapy approaches. These are:

- Music play, live or where appropriate, with sound carrier
- Singing songs for/ with the patient
- Free, theme or rule oriented improvisation (vocal or instrumental)
- Musical role-play

The therapeutic relationship in music therapy is mainly developed on a musical level and needs musical relationship skills – the skill to communicate through music. Examples are the playing for the patient, the empathetic accompaniment of songs, the improvised dialogue, or the group improvisation. The music therapy relationship develops with the help of a repertoire of music-oriented approaches that, modified according the specific process, are offered to the patients.

The necessary competences will be conveyed in class through

- Improvising, musically free and with guidelines like bourdon or cadence structures,

- Vocal and song related competences (quality of the voice, song repertoire, spontaneous singing and instrumental accompaniment of songs),

- Multi-instrumental expressiveness,

- Technical competences on piano and guitar (song accompaniment) as important therapeutic instruments

- Competences in the play of rhythmic instruments

Such lessons not only include manual skills and artistic-pedagogical elements, but also the mediation of an attitude. Previously learned musical competences will initially be placed in service of music intuition and inspiration. This first step is about the acquisition of an inner attitude that enables the experience of music originally, which is used for the interaction between musical ideas and creative actions in a range of unconscious and conscious compositions. Improvisation is conveyed as a spontaneous, symbolizing expression and a non-verbal interaction possibility.

The student is offered a variety of specific practical music learning experiences, for example in the form of solos, duos or partner play, group exercises and role-play, or experimental music actions. Feedback from the group seems a good way to develop or discover implicit and intuitive understanding of possible meanings of non-verbal, acoustic expressive, and interactive behaviour.

Didactically, this, for example, begins with a freely improvised, simple, unisonous, sequence of notes. Melodies of two players later encounter and influence each other alternatively and synchronically, which is then followed by improvisations of more players. A pulsation between dissonance and consonance, between personal and interpersonal join into a new inner hearing experience. As a next step, imagination (such as natural moods, images, and abstract terms) and music structures are experimented on. It is important to learn to hear simple cadences or harmonic functions and then transpose them into various keys. This is not only important for the spontaneous accompaniment of songs, but also for the melodic experiments of the client.

In order to use songs in music therapy, one needs knowledge of how to perform, arrange, and possibly rehearse songs from different times and of different styles. One should be able to accompany simple songs in the name of responding to the patient. The combination of songs, dance, and playing is important for the practical work in various clinical areas.

Training and use of the voice as the instrument closest to the body is important for spontaneous sounding for patients next to the vocal improvisation of songs. Vocal training and speech training promote the awareness for the handling of one's own voice. Body and breath awareness are also the bases, which is important for receptive music therapy. The conscious integration of the body in peace and in movement is a central therapeutic factor.

Rhythm is a central element in music therapy. Schooling in various percussion instruments is therefore essential. Rhythmic competence and empathetic synchronization are carrying and structuring elements in the music therapy relationship. Both the learning of play techniques and the rhythmic, improvisatory elements will be practiced.

Songs and several music therapy improvisations will be tested and practiced during active approaches. Free or musically structured improvisation will not be carried out and reflected after artistic criteria but with regard to music therapeutic relationship formation. The students learn different rules, test improvisations for certain non-musical guidelines like themes of pictures and reflect these with regard to clinical practice. The improvised approach applies to the receptive approach as well when something is played "live". The playing of monotonic instruments (monochord, sound bowl, gong, etc.) is the most elementary approach here. The therapist can furthermore improvise playing any instrument that he or she feels expressive and confident with for the patient. The possible settings are lying down, sitting, standing, movement, and even dance.

Another starting point for the work with students is the musical application of psychotherapeutic techniques like holding, supporting, provoking, and confronting. Interventions like "secure carrying", "supporting walking attempts through presence" or "to bring the other person out of their shell" are performed on the basis of the acquired musical skills. Additionally, patient-therapist and therapist-group role-play are good didactic possibilities to try out (Timmermann, 2012, p. 55 ff.).

At the end of the programme, graduates are able to offer, and carry out, all music therapy approaches confidently and relation-competent.

6. Experiential learning, music therapy self-experience

Being a music therapist requires reflective relation skills. Self-experience in the form of training therapy as single or group music therapy is an integral part of our curriculum and leads to the according personal qualifications. Personal development within the new and therapeutic method to learn differs from the pure self-experience in terms of therapeutic treatment. The training therapy accompanies the students on the path of a changed self-experience and self-reflection in preparation for their therapeutic role with the application of a medium, with a different function that is not yet familiar to most: music and its elements, but also possibly touches own "blind spots". In individual cases, it is suggested to take a break from the training therapy and consider treatment where such "blind spots" are possibly pushed to the fore and make it increasingly harder to focus on the medium and the patient. In such cases, and with agreement of the student, reconciliation will take place between the chief instructors and the training therapist

The programme in Augsburg expects 120 sessions of group therapy training and 100 sessions of single therapy training. The group therapy is integrated into teaching blocks, the single therapy is to be done externally. Training therapists are colleagues qualified by the German music therapy association.

As a further developmental and reflective supporting element, supervision is included in our curriculum in order to work on professional and personal development both with regard to the patient and to music therapy techniques. "Supervision is especially described in retrospect as an important influence by therapists" (Willutzki et al., 2006, p. 26). Supervision is mainly carried out externally next to the internship and additionally during a curricular event with the chief instructors ("Seminar for Support During Internships"). The debriefing sessions with the music therapist who is in charge of the internship are a further supervision element.

7. Evaluation procedures concerning quality of teaching

Until now, the evaluation of our programme has not been included in the evaluation of the whole university. On the one hand, the university-wide evaluation was developed for undergraduate studies, on the other hand, the evaluations of students who have already completed their basic studies and who are on a Masters programme could be more differentiated. Questions concerning the professional relevance of a programme should especially be asked in a field like music therapy. During the evaluation, students are encouraged to give constructive criticism in the sense of wishes and suggestions for changes.

Currently, we are evaluating in a pilot phase as to whether it makes sense to have a special, individual, evaluation for our Masters programme in a university context. The evaluation focuses on the main teaching modules such as music therapy praxeology and theory, practical lesson contents, music therapy research as well as foundation of psychotherapy. It includes both the evaluation of the modules and the evaluation of the lecturers.

We believe that, in addition, an integrated, evaluation structure of the whole university that takes music therapy in Augsburg into account, as well as a comparable evaluation of music therapy Masters programmes in Germany, or even in Europe, could be beneficial, regardless of our current actions. One must consider, however, that the course contents vary, even in Germany.

8. PhD Programme

In 2008, the promotion regulation at the University of Augsburg was expanded to include music therapy. Even those possessing a music therapy degree from a technical college are allowed to do their doctorate at the University of Augsburg in music therapy if their grade point average is at least 1.5. Twice a year there will be a doctoral colloquium in which all doctorates come together in order to present the current status of their promotion as well as critically reflect on their work with the two chief instructors. This happens in addition to the individual mentoring.

9. References

Schmidt, H.U., & Timmermann, T. (Eds.). (2012). *Symbolisierungen in Musik, Kunst und Therapie – präverbal, nonverbal, verbal, transverbal* [Symbolisations in music, arts, and therapy – preverbal, nonverbal, verbal, transverbal]. Wiesbaden: Reichert.

Timmermann, T. (2004). *Tiefenpsychologisch orientierte Musiktherapie* [Psychodynamic oriented music therapy] (2nd ed.). Wiesbaden: Reichert.

Timmermann, T. (2012). Praxeologie [Praxeology]. In H.H. Decker-Voigt, D. Oberegelsbacher, & T. Timmermann (Eds.), *Lehrbuch Musiktherapie* (pp. 55-65). Munich: Reinhardt UTB.

Timmermann, T. (2014). Musikalische Kompetenzen von Musiktherapeuten – Voraussetzungen und Ausbildungsaspekte [Musical competences of music therapists – Requirements and aspects of training]. *Musiktherapeutische Umschau, 35*(3), 220-228.

Willutzki, U., Orlinsky, D., Cierpka, M., Ambühl, H., Laireiter, A.R., Meyerberg, J., et al. (2006). WIR – Daten über uns. Psychotherapeuten in Deutschland, Österreich und der Schweiz [WE – data about us. Psychotherapists in Germany, Austria, and Switzerland]. In O. Kernberg, B. Dulz, & J. Eckert (Eds.), *WIR: Psychotherapeuten*. Stuttgart: Schattauer.

Winnicott, D.W. (1984). *Reifungsprozesse und fördernde Umwelt* [Maturational Processes and the Facilitating Environment: Studies in the Theory of Emotional Development]. Frankfurt: Fischer. (Original work published 1965)

8   Ferrara, Italy

Ferdinando Suvini

©Ferdinando Suvini

©Ferdinando Suvini

Department of Music Therapy
Conservatorio of Music Girolamo Frescobaldi of Ferrara
www.conservatorioferrara.it

Part-time MA Music Therapy Programme
Conservatorio of Music Girolamo Frescobaldi of Ferrara, ITA

FACT SHEET

Institution:	Conservatorio di Musica Girolamo Frescobaldi di Ferrara, Italy
Programme Head:	Prof. Paolo Biagini
Study Period:	2 years
ECTS Credits:	120
Number of students:	Max. 20 per study group
Teaching personnel capacities:	Musical education involving internal Professor of the Conservatorium (full Professors); Music Therapy: annual professional contract to free lance MT; Psychological and medical education: annual professional contract with University Professors or Medical Doctors (Hospital)
Tuition Fee:	1,000 € per year
Target Group/ Addressees:	Professionals in suitable occupations (e.g. music pedagogues, doctors, psychologists, social workers)
Admission Requirements:	BA- or an equivalent degree in health care, humanistic, or psychology and 3 years of theoretical and practical music
Language of Instruction:	Italian
Type:	Part-time Programme with Masters Degree
Academic Degree:	Master of Music Therapy (MA)
Occupational Title:	Music Therapist

The following link provides further information: www.conservatorioferrara.it

1. Background: Developments, theories, and philosophy

The theoretic background models of music therapy can be found within the extensive literature about the early interactions between mother and baby, that is, a field which describes the link between non-verbal and pre-verbal aspects of communication and the expression of emotions.

The deep connection between music and communication lies right in the presence of similar constituent elements in interaction and musical language such as rhythm, repetition, intensity and form.

These elements are also defined by many authors as narrativity, pulse and melodic quality (Malloch & Trevarthen, 2009).

Moreover, in the early relationships between mother and baby it is possible to identify the presence of particular moments defined as affective tunings, which allow for a direct and deep communication of the emotional states (Stern, 1987).

The professional music therapist operates on this ground creating the relationship with the patient by means of gestures, sounds, intensity, rhythms and melodic performances with the intention to make it possible to share emotional states. This way of sharing is favoured and carried by the use of some techniques that every time prove to be the most appropriate with regard to the patient's needs. Such techniques may entail both the active use of musical instruments for free, guided or theme improvisations and the practice of listening to musical pieces from different repertoires (Bruscia, 1987).

By means of the different techniques, the professional music therapist favours the translation of the patient's emotional experience into a sound-musical output; so, it becomes possible to observe an analogical similarity between the musical elements and the regulation of the emotional experience forming the symbolic space of intervention for art therapies (Ricci Bitti, 1998).

It is right within this symbolic space that the transition from the expression of emotions to reflection is actually facilitated in the patient, together with the re-elaboration of the emotional experience (Mancia, 2002).

Thanks to such reflection, the emotions experienced by the patient are placed in a space-time dimension giving a meaning to them. For these reasons the use of music therapy can prove appropriate particularly for those patients having troubles in using verbal language, in case there are specific deficits or relational-type problems which make it difficult or impossible to resort to verbal language in order to identify one's own experience and give voice to one's own suffering.

Music therapy is applied in treatment centres with the purpose of promoting the health of the person (Bruscia, 1998).

It is important to highlight how such purpose can be arranged with respect to the different needs of the individual and with regard to a specific condition as well. In order to outline more precisely the achievable purposes of music therapy, it is crucial to stress that this intervention is aimed to offer the patient musical and relational experiences within various dimensions: physical-sensorial, space-time, empathic, relational, communicative and elaborative.

Those experiences which connect music with the sense of the subjective past are essentially the focus of the music therapeutic intervention.

The professional music therapist promotes a better psycho-physical integration of personality with reference to emotional dynamics so as to reach the symbolic dimension of the relationship.

The projects of music therapy are conducted with regard to important issues that often emerge during the years of growth, such as psycho-intellectual disorders, behavioral disorders, perceptive-sensorial and neuromotor deficits, as well as other issues that are very far from each other, such as psychiatric disorders, cognitive deterioration and senile dementia, coma and post-coma, oncology and palliative treatments.

For all the situations mentioned above, the specific resource that can be used by the music therapist, is given by the fact of being supplied with a space for listening and non-verbal communication: in this way, it is possible to establish a profound relationship with the patient by means of music and allow sharing complex emotions as well as what is frequently an unutterable suffering (Suvini, Bonfiglioli, Zanchi, Bonanomi & Raglio, 2008).

2. Admission criteria and admission procedures

Admission requirements:

The admission to the second level academic course is restricted to those students having a first level academic certificate, a degree certificate, or a conservatory certificate together with an upper school certificate.

Moreover, students having another equivalent educational qualification obtained abroad and recognized as suitable are admitted as well.

The above-mentioned qualifications must be coherent with the selected course.

There might be a number of debits/credits with regard to the educational path previously concluded.

Admission examination:

In order to be admitted to the Music Therapy Experimental Two-year Course there are some exams that are scheduled as follows:

Written test:

a paper (questionnaire or short report) exemplifying the candidate's general explanations and expectations about the course.

Practical test:

only for candidates without a musical study qualification that has been issued by a Conservatory, a certified Musical Institute or a foreign institution on the same level: Performance of an instrumental or vocal piece chosen by the candidate.

Oral test:

Examination of the fundamental theoretical-harmonic notions of music: signs of musical writing (stave and musical notes), notions of harmony (tonality and modulations).

3. Structure and content of the curriculum

Course content

Planning, carrying out and analyzing complex and articulated clinical interventions require the formation of a professional that has completed a reliable and well-organized educational course.

The professional competence of a music therapist is expressed through the capacity of applying one's knowledge to the musical, music therapeutic, psychological and medical areas.

Therefore, the educational process of the professional music therapist is structured into the following four levels:

1. To know: acquisition of notions derived from those disciplines that contribute to the music-therapeutic knowledge;
2. To know how to do: acquisition of practical competence and abilities that are necessary to plan a work project as well as to control and live a music-therapeutic relationship in accordance with the needs of the patient, of the music therapist and the common project;
3. To know how to be: development of a personal awareness within the sound and musical relationship. Acquisition of abilities of auto-observation and auto-analysis;
4. To know how to share: development of the ability to employ one's competence within the social and organizational environments.

The Music Therapy Two-year Course offers theoretical knowledge and practical competence that are specific to music therapy. It is intended to acquaint everyone with all the aspects of the complex and delicate work of the professional music therapist in contact with particularly demanding situations.

Reading the medical record, gathering data, preparing the setting for the session of music therapy, meeting the doctor and the relatives, meeting the rehabilitative team, taking minutes and drawing up the final observations.

Moreover, throughout the educational course a work on oneself is expected to take place (self-experience), which is meant to enable the elaboration of the themes emerged during the work, of the emotional impact with serious pathologies and a follow-up path of one's own personal past.

Objectives of the educational course:

- To form a professional identity that is very definite for knowledge, competence, quality and area of intervention;
- To supply professional musical competences;
- To define a therapeutic identity based on the knowledge of the theoretical material about the psychological subjects.
- To teach the musical and clinical techniques specific to the discipline.
- To cope with the knowledge of one's own personal dynamics.
- To develop and investigate evaluation capacities of the complex dynamics that are set in motion over the course of a relation of help;
- To elaborate a project of intervention and attendant protocols;
- To qualify music therapy as a rigorous discipline, by providing the students with an adequate cultural, personal preparation that is also associated to practical application;

Specific objectives of individual areas

Objectives Musical Area

- The programme is aimed to let the students acquire notions and competences concerning the sound/musical language that are specific to those who deal with music therapy.
- To understand the characteristics of one's own musicality and sound identity;
- To consciously develop one's own musical expressiveness and creativity;
- To improve the ability to communicate and interact by means of non-verbal languages with particular reference to sound and music;
- To acquire the abilities of decoding, reading and analyzing the sound/musical language.

Objectives Music Therapy Area

The programme broaches the historical profile and the scientific premises of Italian music therapy and the international one concerning the methodological and technical issues (planning, modality of observation, intervention, test and evaluation of the results), in order to conduct simulations and analysis of some clinical cases by means of self-centring work groups and laboratories.

Objectives Psychological Area

The programme is aimed to the acquisition of notions from the psychological area that are oriented towards the observation so as to develop communicative and re-lational competences as most effective and conscious as possible.

Objectives Medical Area

The programme is aimed to the acquisition of knowledge of the main patholo-gies treated in the music therapy environment. The strategies of treatment and fol-low-up that are offered serve the purpose of developing professional knowledge and competences in order to promote the integration of the music therapist into a teamwork, with particular reference to the preventive and rehabilitative area.

Final Examination

The final examination requires the elaboration, presentation and discussion of a thesis about a subject that has been previously arranged with a Teacher of the Course, who will have the role of Mentor of the paper itself. The subject of the Thesis is focused on the training clinical experience.

4. Clinical training, internships

Clinical training: to take the first steps in the clinical approach to the patient through a coached and guided method. Get to know in person the pathologies, one's own reactions, improve one's own abilities. To experience the methods of documentation and the interdisciplinary collaboration. Gather material for the thesis.

Individual, group and small groups tutoring.

Objectives: to coach and guide the student along the course and towards the ob-jectives of the clinical training. To support them in the difficulties and lead them to find their own personal style of intervention. To guide them in writing up the thesis.

The internships include at least 250 hours in total, which are structured as:

- internship instructor, participating in team meetings

- work with patients (alone and in groups)

- tutoring and supervision

- preparation, reworking, and documentation

5. Overview of the Structure of the Programme

The programme is designed to be a two-year, part-time, that takes place in
I YEAR:
13 weekend (15 hours each) + 3 intensive weeks (40 hours each = 315 total hours).
II YEAR:
13 weekend (15 hours each) + 3 intensive weeks (40 hours each) = 309 hours).

Academic Programme	1st Year CH	CP	E/ID	2nd Year CH	CP	E/ID
MUSIC THERAPY AREA						
Basic educational activities						
Theory of Music Therapy	60	10	Yes	48	8	Yes
Music therapeutic listening	30	5	Yes	24	4	Yes
Music Therapy Improvisation	=	=	=	24	2	ID
Music Therapy in rehabilitation	28	4	Yes	=	=	=
Work on oneself (self-experience)	36	6	Yes	36	6	Yes
Tutoring – analysis of experiences	40	8	Yes	35	7	Yes
Applied Music Therapy	12	4	ID	12	4	ID
MUSICAL AREA						
Musical Performance	=	=	ID	8	1	ID
Musical Informatics	12	2	Yes	=	=	=
MEDICAL PSYCHOLOGICAL AREA						
Neurology	12	2	Yes			
Psychopathology	=	=	=	12	2	Yes
Neuropsychology	=	=	=	12	2	Yes
Psychoacustic	8	1	Yes	=	=	=
Team work	=	=	=	24	2	ID
Rehabilitative Medicine	14	2	Yes	=	=	=
Acquired brain injury	12	2	Yes	=	=	=
Psychological aspects follow-up	=	=	=	12	2	ID
Hospitalization	=	=	=	24	2	ID
General psychology	12	2	Yes	=	=	=
Psychology of the elderly	=	=	=	6	1	ID

Academic Programme	1st Year CH	CP	E/ID	2nd Year CH	CP	E/ID
OTHER SUBJECTS						
First aid	6	1	ID			
Foreign language	=	=	=	12	2	Yes
Training	33	11	ID	36	6	ID
Volunteer training				150		
Final Exam	=	=	=	=	10	=
Total hours / Credits / Exams	315	60	-	475	61	-

CH (contact hours): events to complete; (E: examen for each teaching; ID: idoneity for each teaching); CP (credit points)

6. Evaluation procedures concerning quality of teaching

The evaluation of the Two-Year Postgraduate Course of Music Therapy falls within the parameters used by the Conservatory for the evaluation of the internal academic courses offered.

The evaluation is based on specific questionnaires about aspects concerning the organizational aspects as well as the specific contents of the course.

Every teacher is evaluated for specific aspects, such as the capacity of conducting, the specificity of the lessons, the educational and expository capacities, clearness, coherence as well as the capacity to listen and manage the relations.

7. References

Bruscia, K.E. (1987). *Improvisational models of music therapy*. Ismez: Roma.

Bruscia, K.E. (1998). *Defining music therapy* (2nd ed.). Gilsum, NH: Barcelona Publishers.

Mancia, M. (2002). Psicoanalisi e forme musicali [Psychoanalysis and musical Form]. In V. Volterra (Ed.), *Melanconia e musica. Creatività e sofferenza mentale* [Melancholy and music. Creativity and mental disease] (pp. 88-95). Milano: Franco Angeli.

Malloch, S., & Trevarthen, C. (Eds.). (2009). *Communicative musicality: Exploring the basis of human companionship*. Oxford: Oxford University Press.

Ricci Bitti, P.E. (Ed.). (1998). *Regolazione delle emozioni e artiterapie* [Emotional regulation and arts therapy]. Roma: Carocci Editore.

Stern, D.N. (1987). *Il mondo interpersonale del bambino* [The interpersonal world of the infant]. Torino: Boringhieri. (Original work published 1979)

Suvini, F., Bonfiglioli, L., Zanchi, B., Bonanomi, C., & Raglio, A.(2008). Musicoterapia, realtà e prospettive di una professione [Music therapy: The state of art of a profession]. *Rivista Italiana Pediatria, ACP 15*(4), 186-188.

9   Liepaja, Latvia

Katie Roth and Mirdza Paipare

©Kristine Timermane

©Ojars Saulatis

Postgraduate Music Therapy Programme
University of Liepaja
http://www.liepu.lv/lv/608/muzikas-terapija

Part-time Postgraduate Music Therapy Programme
University of Liepaja, LVA

FACT SHEET

Institution:	University of Liepaja, Latvia
Programme Head:	Docent (Associate Professor) Mirdza Paipare M.A. Music, M.A. Health Care
Study Period:	6 semesters
ECTS Credits:	150
Number of students:	10-12 per study group
Teaching personnel capacities:	Programme Director, Lectureships
Tuition Fee:	1,410 € per year
Target Group/ Addressees:	Professionals in suitable occupations (e.g., music teachers, musicians, kindergarten teachers, psychologists, social workers)
Admission Requirements:	BA or equivalent degree, keyboard and vocal improvisation test, interview regarding motivation and suitability, relevant experiences with children and/or adults with special needs. Students are required to undertake their own therapy over the duration of the course (50 hours individual and 100 hours group therapy)
Language of Instruction:	Latvian (English and German)
Type:	Part-time Programme with Master's Degree
Academic Degree:	Professional Master's Degree (MA) in Health Care
Occupational Title:	Arts Therapist in Music Therapy

The following link provides further information:
http://www.liepu.lv/lv/608/muzikas-terapija

1. Background: Developments, theories, and philosophy

The foundational principle, taken from Nordoff-Robbins' Creative Music Therapy, is that of the 'music child' or 'music person'. This is defined as "the individualized musicality inborn in each child which responds to musical experience, finds it meaningful and engaging, remembers music, and enjoys some form of musical expression" (Nordoff & Robbins, 1977, p. 1). The focus is on music as a healing element in its own right, with only sparing use of verbal processing.

Two main movements of humanistic philosophy and psychology formed the foundation of Creative Music Therapy. The first was anthroposophy, which fosters inner development through the use of imagination, inspiration and intuition. The defining anthroposophical principles which influenced Nordoff and Robbins are those of a deep reverence and respect for the inner life, the significance of every individual, and the existence of a "musical self" in every human being (McDermott, 1992).

The second movement was Abraham Maslow's humanistic psychology, which posits that every human being has a strong drive to realise their potential and to activate their positive strengths and skills. The focus is on the inner resources within people for growth and healing, rather than concentrating on symptoms of sickness and dysfunction. The concept of peak experience, as an intense, joyful, awe-inspiring moment that releases creative energy and a sense of deep connection with other humans and transcendental reality, is also significant in Creative Music Therapy. Peak experiences can be inspired by exposure to music and can be therapeutic in the way they increase potential for free will, self-determination and empathy (Wigram, Pedersen & Bonde, 2002).

The neuro-physiological approach to music therapy is closely connected to Nordoff-Robbins' Creative Music Therapy and is strongly emphasised in the course at Liepaja University. This involves developing the connections between the two hemispheres of the brain, hand-mouth co-ordination, bilateral motor co-ordination and pitch differentiation, as the therapist synchronises with the client's movements, instrumental play and vocalisations (Paipare, 2011).

Whilst the course was originally founded solely on principles of Creative Music Therapy, and geared towards work with children who have physical and mental handicaps, over time elements of psychodynamic theory have been added to the curriculum. Of particular relevance is the work of the psychologist Daniel Stern, including the concepts of forms of vitality and intersubjectivity (Stern, 1985, 2010).

Stern's research, carried out over a number of decades, has identified five 'vitality forms' of "movement, time, force, space, and intention/directionality" (Stern, 2010, p. 4) which are evident in human interaction from the earliest days of life. Stern demonstrates how these are manifested in both verbal and non-verbal interaction, and are essential for developing a sense of self in relationship with others. He cites improvisational music therapy as an example of a powerful clinical intervention that facilitates these forms, referring to Wigram's (2004) techniques of improvisation (see Musical Training section below for more detail). These techniques also contribute to the development of intersubjectivity, which may be defined very simply as the experience of shared *emotion*, shared *attention* and shared *intention*. We experience ourselves in relationship with others, in which each person's experience has an impact on the experience of the other. Such reciprocal experiences are fundamental to human life – the knowing of ourselves through being experienced by another (Stern, 1985, 2010; Trevarthen, 1980).

Whilst the humanistic, psychodynamic and neurophysiological approaches outlined above form the theoretical foundation of the programme in Liepaja, the course is also influenced by the tendency in the Latvian arts therapy community towards an integrative-eclectic approach (Krevica, 2011). This approach acknowledges the diverse roots of Music Therapy, which include the arts, psychoanalysis, humanistic psychotherapies and education. It also values the wide range of evidence-based practice in music therapy worldwide, including developmental, behavioural, cognitive, artistic/creative, active/directive, family/systemic, neuro-scientific, transpersonal and community-based approaches (Karkou & Sanderson, 2006). The key in the integrative-eclectic approach is that specific practices drawn from various therapeutic perspectives are applied with particular client groups, in particular settings, with a clear rationale for their use. Music therapists must have a good understanding of the theoretical foundations, indications, contra-indications and limitations of the interventions they use, and be sure that the underlying concepts are not in contradiction with each other (Paipare, 2013).

In summary, the course at Liepaja University aims to give students a firm foundation in Creative Music Therapy, based on humanistic and neuro-physiological principles, with selected elements of psychodynamic theory, especially those relating to Daniel Stern's work on forms of vitality and intersubjectivity. In addition, students are made aware of other traditions and theories which may be beneficial to their work, and encouraged to supplement their basic training in these areas, according to the demands of their emerging clinical practice.

2. Admission criteria and admission procedures

Prospective students must have a BA or equivalent degree in a relevant discipline, such as music performance, music education, psychology, social work, special education or early years education. They must also have relevant experience of work with children and/or adults with special needs. At interview, prospective students must demonstrate competent musical skills at the piano, on percussion instruments and vocally. They need to demonstrate their potential improvisatory skills in free improvisation tests in each of these areas. These tests include both playing individually and taking the role of therapist in an improvisation, with one of the interviewers taking the role of the client. The prospective student's motivation and suitability is also assessed in an interview about the personal and professional experiences which have led them to apply for the course. There is no requirement for personal therapy or an observation placement before the start of the course. Students are required to undertake their own therapy over the duration of the course (50 hours individual and 100 hours group therapy), and an observation placement forms part of the first year programme.

The language of instruction is Latvian. All practical work and presentations must be done in Latvian. However students may, by prior agreement with lecturers, submit written work in English or German instead of Latvian.

3. Structure and content of the curriculum

Overview of the Structure of the Programme

The programme is a three-year (6-semester), part-time, postgraduate programme that takes place over a total of 11 study blocks of 6 days each, as shown below:

1st Year	5 study blocks	232 contact hours
2nd Year	5 study blocks	128 contact hours
3rd Year	1 study block	16 contact hours

Additionally, there are events that students are expected to organise themselves:

1st Year	4-week observation placement
2nd Year	6-week field-learning placement with children and young people
	6-week field-learning placement with adults
	2-week practical research and evaluation placement
3rd Year	4-week clinical practice placement
	4-week research work placement

Students are also required to organise 50 hours of individual and 100 hours of group therapy for themselves over the three years of the programme.

Course Contents

The course components have been chosen to provide students with sufficient depth and breadth of knowledge and skills for a beginning music therapist. These include courses that focus specifically on music therapy, as well as those from related disciplines:

	CP	CH	Indepen-dent Study
Music Therapy Specific Courses			
Introduction to Music Therapy	6	32	128
Theories and Concepts of Music Therapy	3	16	64
Keyboard Improvisation	3	16	64
Movement and Vocal Improvisation	3	16	64
Research and Evaluation Techniques in Music Therapy	3	16	64
Music Therapy Methodology with Children and Young People	3	16	64
Music Therapy Methodology with Adults	3	16	64
Scientific Research in Music Therapy	3	16	64
Practical Research in Music Therapy	3	16	64
Total	30	16	640
Courses from Related Disciplines			
Individual and Group Counselling Skills	6	32	128
Special Education and Psychology	3	16	64
Developmental Psychology	3	16	64
Social Psychology	3	16	64
Clinical Psychology	3	16	64
Communication Psychology	3	16	64
Human Anatomy and Physiology	3	16	64
Neurophysiology	3	16	64
Introduction to Psychotherapy	3	16	64
Psychiatry and Psychosomatic Medicine	3	16	64
First Aid	3	16	64
Munich Functional Development Diagnostics	1,5	8	32
Supervision	1,5	8	32
Voice Development or Speech Therapy	1,5	8	32
Dance and Movement Therapy	1,5	8	32
Total	42	224	896

In addition, 35 credit points are awarded for the master's thesis and 3 for the quali-fication exam. A further 39 credit points are awarded for practice placements, as described in the next section. In total, there are 150 ECTS credit points, 384 con-tact hours, and 1536 hours of independent study.

4. Clinical training, internships

The courses on Special Education, Neurophysiology and Voice Development include field visits to special schools, homes for children with disabilities and hospital clinics. These visits provide opportunities for students to ground their theoretical lectures in real-world situations, under the guidance of lecturers.

The 1st Year 4-week observation placement requires students to observe certified music therapists working with both individuals and groups. They complete detailed, structured reports of their observations for presentation to their study group.

In the 2nd Year, there are two 6-week field-learning placements, one with children and young people and one with adults. During both placements, students work with both an individual and a group, and produce detailed case studies of their work. There is also a 2-week practical research and evaluation element to these field placements, in which students are required to select and implement assessment and evaluation instruments specifically designed for music therapy.

In the 3rd Year, the clinical practice placement and research study placements are intended for students to focus on the area of interest which will form the basis of their master's thesis. They work with clients in a setting of their choice, arranging their own supervision and gathering research data, in consultation with their thesis director.

5. Musical training

The musical training element of the course includes keyboard and vocal skills, as well as work on a wide range of percussion instruments. Across all three areas, the emphasis is on developing existing skills in order to apply them to the new professional demands of therapy, as opposed to performance or teaching, from which musical backgrounds many students come. Some students come with a high level of accomplishment in performance on their main instrument, but never having experienced free improvisation.

Others begin the course with a feeling of uncertainty about their vocal or keyboard abilities. In either case, students need the opportunity to experiment in a supportive environment, to take risks in front of their peers and to listen carefully to their own and each other's playing, as they try out a range of improvisational techniques individually, in pairs and in groups. In this environment, students can experience the roles of both therapist and client, and give each other feedback about how their playing is perceived by others.

The basic skills of keyboard improvisation as explained by Wigram (2004) form the basis of the training in this area. Students learn how to use play rules, pulsed and non-pulsed playing, chordal, melodic, dissonant and atonal improvisation. Having gained a foundation in these basic improvisational skills, students begin to utilise them in the therapeutic methods of mirroring, matching, empathic improvisation, grounding, holding, containing, dialoguing and accompanying. The techniques of 'seductive', limbo and overlap transitions are then added to the improvisational 'toolkit' available for students' use. Other keyboard techniques, such as playing a well-known folk song, varying the key, tempo, meter, pulse and style of accompaniment, are also practised.

Students are encouraged to familiarise themselves with using their voices in a wide range of vocalisation techniques. Whilst Latvia has a strong tradition of choral singing, many students have never had the opportunity to experiment freely with their voices, moving beyond the limitations of singing pre-composed songs 'correctly'. In order to use their voices effectively as therapists, they often need to work through childhood experiences in school singing lessons, and learn to use their voices with creative freedom. Furthermore, students with professional vocal training may need to recognise that their singing expertise might be off-putting for clients who feel unsure about their own voices. They need to learn how to sing in a less 'polished' way, so as to encourage clients to begin to use their voices with freedom and authenticity.

A wide range of percussion instruments is available for students' use. Historically, in Latvia, there has been a strong emphasis on singing, traditional notation and music history in school music lessons (Stramkale, 2008; Valsts Izglītības Satura Centrs, 2005; Zariņš, 2003). This means that many students have had limited access to such instruments, and may never have experienced group composition or improvisation. Therefore, students are given many opportunities to experiment with these instruments in both free and more structured activities.

6. Experiential learning, music therapy self-experience

Ongoing personal and professional growth is essential for every therapist at every stage of their career. In Liepaja we aim to establish the habits of personal therapy and professional supervision for every student, ensuring that they understand and value the function and significance of both these forms of self-reflection.

Supervision, both individually and in a group, is viewed as a collaborative work, with the aim of examining, understanding and developing the process of the supervisee's work with clients (Merry, 1999). The behaviour, attitudes and feelings of not only the client, but also the therapist, and how these elements are played out in their interaction, must be examined. Thus the therapist's own needs and issues are relevant to the process of supervision insofar as they relate to their professional work. However, supervision always has as its agenda the enhancement of clinical knowledge, skills, attitudes and performance. Personal therapy, on the other hand, has no agenda other than the needs and goals of the client, in this case the student therapist. For many trainee therapists, a key goal is that of self-awareness, which allows them to identify the intra- and inter-personal issues which may affect their emotional and psychological health as they enter a profession which demands high levels of personal maturity. For others, personal therapy provides necessary support during the potentially stressful process of studying and acquiring a new profession (Malikiosi-Loizos, 2013).

The programme in Liepaja expects students to participate in 100 sessions of group therapy and 50 sessions of individual therapy. Of the group therapy hours, 50% must be music therapy, conducted by a certified music therapist, with the aim of facilitating professional development in this area, and as a means of understanding group dynamics 'from the inside'. The other 50% may include other types of group therapy, such as psychodrama or other arts therapies, and is intended for the personal growth of the students. Verbal psychotherapy is recommended for individual work. Both group and individual therapy take place externally, in addition to the taught course requirements, and students are responsible for organising this themselves. However, on occasion, a visiting lecturer may offer group therapy as part of a master class or training seminar, and these hours may be counted towards the group requirement.

Group supervision is an integral part of the curriculum, introduced progressively over the three years. Students are introduced to the supervision format after carrying out their observation practice placements in the first year, as they present their observations of another therapist's work to their fellow students, under the supervision of the course director. In the second year, as students undertake their field learning placement, group supervision of students' own work is carried out on a weekly basis. Each student presents a specific case for consideration by the group, under the guidance of either the course director or an experienced external music therapy supervisor. This experience is followed up by a theoretical course on supervision in which each student is required to research and present a specific aspect of the supervision process. In the third year, students are expected to seek external supervision during their clinical practice, either individually or in a group. Another aspect of work with a supervisor during this final year is the requirement to engage in supervision that focuses specifically on the research work undertaken for the master's thesis. Additionally, visiting lecturers from overseas provide opportunities to present cases for supervision in a seminar format, open to all current students, alumni and other practising music therapists.

7. Evaluation procedures concerning quality of teaching

There is a Quality Control System in place at Liepaja University which carries out a multi-faceted annual evaluation of each programme, based on a number of different sources of data. Students complete questionnaires at the end of their first and third years, covering a range of topics. These include availability of resources, relevance of subject matter, usefulness of independent study assignments, practice placements, approachability of teaching staff, and opportunities for overseas exchange visits. A more detailed supplementary questionnaire about quality of teaching gathers information about the structure, comprehensiveness and relevance of courses, as well as inclusion of contemporary issues, problems and research in the field of study. Lecturers' levels of preparation, clarity, organisation, use of audio-visual aids, attitudes towards students, punctuality and presentation styles are also rated.

Graduates complete questionnaires in which they evaluate the theoretical and practical knowledge and skills gained during their university studies in the light of professional demands in their workplaces. The information from these student and graduate questionnaires is collated and discussed in faculty meetings, with the aim of identifying the strengths and weaknesses of each programme. Detailed action and development plans are devised for each subject area in order to solve problems raised by students' responses and to build on the identified strengths. A full report of the results from each annual evaluation is compiled and published on the university website, thus adhering to principles of transparency and accountability.

8. PhD Programme

Currently there is no doctoral programme in Music Therapy available at Liepaja University. Students wishing to further their studies are encouraged to apply to overseas universities offering studies at this level. The course director can assist students in this process, as many links exist with universities in other countries that have older, more established music therapy departments that are able to offer studies at this level.

9. References

Karkou, V., & Sanderson, P. (2006). *Arts therapies: A research based map of the field.* London: Elsevier.

Krevica, E. (2011). Psiholoģijas un psihoterapijas ietekmes mākslu terapijā. [The Influence of Psychology and Psychotherapy on Arts Therapies.] In K. Mārtinsone (Ed.), *Mākslu terapija* [Arts Therapy] (pp. 76-105). Rīga: RaKa.

Malikiosi-Loizos, M. (2013). Personal therapy for future therapists: Reflections on a still debated issue. *The European Journal of Counselling Psychology, 2*(1), 33-50.

McDermott, R.A. (1992). Rudolf Steiner and Anthroposophy. In A. Faivre, J. Needleman, & K. Voss (Eds), *Modern esoteric spirituality* (pp. 288-310). New York: Crossroad.

Merry, T. (1999). *Learning and being in Person-Centred Counselling.* Monmouth: PCCS Books.

Nordoff, P., & Robbins, C. (1977). *Creative music therapy.* New York: John Day.

Paipare, M. (2011). Mūzikas Terapija. [Music Therapy.] In K. Mārtinsone (Ed.), *Mākslu terapija* [Arts Therapy] (pp. 340-373). Rīga: RaKa.

Paipare, M. (2013). Integrative-eclectic music therapy. In K. Kirkland, *International Dictionary of Music Therapy* (1st ed., p. 44). London: Routledge.

Stern, D. (1985). *The interpersonal world of the infant*. New York: Basic Books.

Stern, D. (2010). *Forms of vitality*. Oxford: Oxford University Press.

Stramkale, L. (2008) Mūzika vispārizglītojošā skolā: vēsturiskais un mūsdienu aspekts. [Music at comprehensive school: The historical and present day aspects.] *Latvijas Universitātes Raksti. Pedagoģija un skolotāju izglītība. 741. sējums*. [Latvia University Scientific Papers. Pedagogy and Teacher Education. Volume 741.] (pp. 81-88). Rīga: LU Akadēmiskais apgāds.

Trevarthen, C. (1980). The foundations of intersubjectivity: Development of inter-personal and co-operative understanding in infants. In D. Olsen (Ed.), *The Social Foundations of Language and Thought: Essays in Honour of J. S. Bruner* (316-342). New York: W. W. Norton.

Valsts Izglītības Satura Centrs (2005). *Mūzika 1. - 9. klasei. Pamatizglītības mācību priekšmeta programmas paraugs*. [Music for classes 1st-9th primary education curriculum exemplar]. Rīga: Izglītības un Eksaminācijas Centrs.

Wigram, T. (2004). *Improvisation: Methods and techniques for music therapy clinicians, educators and students*. London: Jessica Kingsley.

Wigram, T., Pedersen I.N., & Bonde, L.O. (2002). *A comprehensive guide to music therapy: Theory, clinical practice, research and training*. London: Jessica Kingsley.

Zariņš, D. (2003). *Mūzikas pedagoģijas pamati*. [Fundamentals of Music Pedagogy.] Rīga: RaKa.

10 Katowice, Poland

Ludwika Konieczna-Nowak

©Marek Bebłot

©Karolina Kacperek

Music Therapy Programme
The Karol Szymanowski Academy of Music, Katowice

www.am.katowice.pl

Full time BA and MA, and Part-time Postgraduate Equivalency Music Therapy Programme

The Karol Szymanowski Academy of Music in Katowice, POL

FACT SHEET

Institution:	The Karol Szymanowski Academy of Music in Katowice
Programme Head:	Dr. Ludwika Konieczna-Nowak
Study Period:	6 semesters BA, 4 semesters MA Music Therapy
	4 semesters Postgraduate Equivalency Music Therapy
ECTS Credits:	180/120/min. 60 (BA/MA/Equivalency)
Number of students:	Max. 6 per study group on BA and MA,
	max 12 on Equivalency course
Teaching personnel	1 Professor, 1 Visiting Professor, 1 Adjunct (PhD),
capacities:	ca. 10 Lecturers
Tuition Fee:	None (BA/MA); approx. 1,600 € for the complete
	Equivalency course (4 semesters)
Target Group/	BA: high school graduates with music competences
Addressees:	MA: music therapy BA's and occasionally BA's in related fields
	Postgraduate Equivalency: professionals (BA's and MA's) in related fields and suitable occupations (e.g. music pedagogues, medical doctors, psychologists, social workers, musicians)
Adm. Requirements:	BA: high school exit exam passed, entrance exams covering musical skills (solfeggio, harmony, vocal and instrumental competences), interview. MA: BA degree in music therapy or related fields, entrance exam covering foundations of music therapy/vocal and instrumental competences. Equivalency: BA or MA in related fields, entrance exams covering interview/vocal and instrumental competences.
Language of Instr.:	Polish (with English option; after individual arrangement)
Type:	Full time BA and MA Programme, Part-time Equivalency
Academic Degree:	Bachelor of Arts, Master of Arts.
Occupational Title:	Music Therapist

The following link provides further information:
http://www.am.katowice.pl/?a=322122_zaklad-muzykoterapii

1. Background: Developments, theories, and philosophy

The theoretical background of the programme based at The Karol Szymanowski Academy of Music in Katowice might be considered eclectic. The educators who created the programme have different backgrounds: from neurologic and behaviourally-oriented music therapists to Nordoff-Robbins and Guided Imagery and Music trained professionals. The idea is to provide students with as broad perspective as possible and enable them to choose the approach that suits their abilities and personality the most, and as such – the approach that is the best for their clients. Given the vast number of frameworks in which music therapy can be provided and reflected on, the students are offered the knowledge and the skills allowing them to make an informed decision as far as their main field of interest is concerned. They are also then encouraged and mentored directly in the chosen area.

The programme covers different therapy philosophies and psychological concepts, including cognitive-behavioural principles as well as humanistic and psychodynamic perspectives. Principles of different models of music therapy are presented, with emphasis on Creative Music Therapy, Behavioural Music Therapy and Neurologic Music Therapy, as well as Polish music therapy achievements (works by Elżbieta Galińska and Maciej Kierył). The discussions pertain to the aspects of *music as therapy* and *music in therapy*, presenting their implications for conducting and analysing the treatment itself as well as its outcomes. The notion that the client is both an individual and a part of the community is emphasized, therefore lots of community music therapy concepts are also being discussed during the courses; the programme also includes projects that integrate different groups in environments not typical for therapeutic actions.

As the programme is being held in the music academy, active music making and its artistic value are deemed important, accompanied by aesthetic reflection. Both creative process and its results are considered potentially therapeutic and important in the treatment. Awareness of historical and current aesthetic concepts, music and emotional expression, symbolic and metaphoric features of music, are important for understanding therapeutic process based in arts. As the future music therapists are taught to use their artistic abilities and experiences, other artistic mediums, such as visual arts, drama or movement expression are also explored during the studies to provide the students with means of self-experience and open them to the possibilities that art brings into everybody's life.

2. Admission criteria and admission procedures

BA level

Required background:
- high school exit exam passed

Suitability individual exam in two parts:
- Music competences:
  - Aural training, harmony, instrumental and voice competences
  - solfeggio – singing a melody (usually from classic or early romantic period literature) a vista, analysing harmonic progression, playing cadences and harmonic modulations on piano, playing chosen piece of music on piano and second instrument (if primary instrument is different than piano), singing song of choice.
- General competences:
  - interview about the motivation and expectations of the applicant

MA level

Required background:
- BA diploma in music therapy (or, sometimes, related areas, such as music education or psychology)

Suitability individual exam in two parts:
- Music competences:
- performing a song with own accompaniment on piano or guitar
- Music therapy theoretical and practical competences:
- oral exam covering theoretical backgrounds of music therapy, its models and their characteristics, techniques with possible applications, and current research achievements.

Equivalency studies

Required background:
- BA or MA diploma in related fields (music education, music psychology, psychology, special education, music, medicine)

Suitability individual exam in two parts:
- Music competences:
- performing a song with own accompaniment on piano or guitar, or performing a song a cappella and playing an instrumental piece
- General competences:
- interview about the motivation and expectations of the applicant

Additional information:

Three levels of studies offered in Katowice are designed for different groups of people, and the differences are reflected in the expectations set on the entrance exams. However, no matter what level they choose, all candidates attend an interview-based exam with an exam board. The board consists of five faculty members (including the head of music therapy, other music therapists and music education instructors).

Students applying for BA level studies are quite young (typically 19 years old), and usually come straight from the secondary music schools. They are well grounded musically, especially instrumentally, but might not have clear goals and ideas regarding the choice of the future professions. The exams for this level cover musical skills that show the potential for future development of professional music therapist and also – thanks to the interview – give information on individual motivations and previous experiences.

Students applying for MA in a vast majority have obtained BA in music therapy. Therefore, they are expected to have advanced music skills, and these are tested simply by performing a song with own accompaniment. The emphasis is not only put on the artistic value of the performance, but also on communicative and social aspects of it as well as the ability to think about the particular song in the therapeutic context. The oral part of the exam that follows usually starts with the question about possible applications of the presented song in the course of the therapy. Both musical features and lyrics are the subject of discussion.

Students at this level should exhibit good knowledge of theoretical and practical issues in music therapy. Typically, each student receives two questions concerning theoretical backgrounds, current trends or practical problems in music therapy. The student is expected not only to present the correct answers but also to be able to elaborate on them, put in individual perspective and share related experiences.

The equivalency course is designed for graduates in related fields. During the exam their motivation and previous educational and professional experiences are discussed. Candidates are also asked about their expectations regarding the course, to make sure if it is possible to meet them in the programme. Musical skills are tested through performance of a song with accompaniment or singing and playing a chosen instrument separately.

3. Structure and content of the curriculum

Music therapy programme is one of the options offered at the music education department of The Karol Szymanowski Academy of Music in Katowice. It is also held in cooperation with the Medical University of Silesia. Thanks to this unique opportunity, BA and MA level studies combine four main blocks: specific music therapy courses, music and music education courses, medical courses, and general academic courses. The equivalency course functions independently. Each of the levels will be described shortly below.

Overview of the structure and content – BA level

The programme is designed to be a three-year (6-semester) full time undergraduate course. The number of hours amounts to 1,800 mandatory classes (contact hours, including clinical hours) plus optional and elective courses (number of optional/elective hours might differ from student to student). It is practically focused on developing clinical music therapy skills with solid theoretical backgrounds, together with good knowledge and skills in music education and basic skills in other art therapies.

The specific *music therapy* courses that are available include:

Theoretical foundations of music therapy (45 h), music therapy techniques (180 h), clinical applications of music therapy (150 h – 75 in class and 75 in "the field" at a third-party institution, with a supervisor), music therapy principles and practices (45 h), piano improvisation and accompaniment in music therapy (30 h).

Additional courses designed for music therapy students only are as follows:

Psychotherapy (15 h), art therapy (135 h), drama therapy (60 h), music and movement (30 h).

Music and music education courses include:

Piano (30 h – individual consultations), guitar (30 h – small groups), voice (20 h), aural training (60 h), harmony (30 h), orchestration (30 h), music literature (30 h), conducting (30 h), music in schools (15 h), Orff workshops (60 h), Kodaly workshops (60 h).

Medical courses:

Anatomy (10 h), first aid (5 h), psychiatry and psychopathology (15 h).

General academic courses combine the subjects that are obligatory in Polish higher education system, including e.g. English language, philosophy, IT.

Overview of the structure and content – MA level

The programme is designed to be a two-year (4-semester) full time course. The number of hours is ca. 650 of obligatory classes (including clinical hours) plus optional/elective courses (number of optional and elective hours might differ from student to student). This advanced programme is focused on further development of music therapists (who are practically qualified professionals having obtained BA in this discipline) with courses targeted on specific populations, building decent research skills and extensive awareness of current literature and developing deeper personal insights.

The specific *music therapy courses* at this level include:

Current trends in music therapy (with one semester focused on research methodology only – 75 h), music therapy in early intervention (15 h), music therapy in special education (15 h), music therapy in intellectual disability (15 h), music therapy in hearing impairments (15 h), music therapy in visual impairments (15 h), music therapy in forensic services (15 h), music therapy in psychiatry (15 h), music therapy in gerontology (15 h). Each of these specific courses is led by lecturers with current clinical experience in working with the given population. Thanks to this specialization, students gather knowledge on up to date literature, research findings, problems and practical tips regarding specific group of music therapy beneficiates. On MA level, students are responsible for finding a place for internship (135 h) and instead of individual supervision, there are group meetings held in order to discuss their experiences.

Music and music education courses include:

Music pedagogy (30 h), psychology of music (15 h), composition and arrangement (30 h)

Medical courses:

Physiotherapy (15 h), paediatrics (15 h), psychiatry (15 h), psychotherapy (15 h). The last two courses are continuation of those started on BA level.

General academic courses combine the subjects that are obligatory in Polish higher education system, including ethics and modern philosophy.

Overview of the structure and content – Equivalency programme

This programme is designed to be a two-year (4-semester) part-time course. The number of hours is 420 of obligatory classes (including clinical hours) and there are no optional or elective classes. It takes place on weekends (Saturdays and Sundays), 9 times a year (once a month, from October to June). Target groups include professionals from related disciplines, who wish to expand their competences to music therapy. As they are coming from different backgrounds and their skills vary, it is challenging to meet the needs of all students in group classes. Therefore lecturers are flexible and allow for more individualized educational process, requiring different times of preparations from students with different backgrounds. The courses offered include, for example: introduction to music therapy (10 h), music therapy techniques (15 h), clinical applications of music therapy (60 h), music therapy improvisation (15 h), Orff workshops (10 h), art therapy (25 h), psychology (20 h), elements of psychotherapy (20 h). During the equivalency course, each student has to complete 60 hours of supervised clinical work.

International Cooperation

Besides the courses listed in the curriculum, the music therapy programme in Katowice is a vivid place with truly international atmosphere. In terms of international cooperation that has found a permanent place in Katowice, it is important to mention that:

Dr. Barbara Wheeler is a visiting professor, who currently teaches one course at the BA level and one at the MA level;

thanks to the bilateral agreement between The Karol Szymanowski Academy of Music and School of Music, University of Louisville (USA) exchange of students and teachers takes place practically every year. Groups of students and faculty members take part in short visits and individual students may participate in a semester-long exchange.

Additionally, every year Katowice hosts renowned music therapy guests, such as: Clive Robbins (in 2010), Felicity Baker, Darcy DeLoach, Petra Kern, Sarah Johnson, Wendy Magee, Amelia Oldfield, Simon Procter.

4. Clinical training, internships

Clinical practice for students is structured differently, depending on the level of studies.

On BA level, each student is required to spend at least one hour a week in one of the institutions providing music therapy services, supervised by a professional music therapist during their work in the field. The practice starts from the second semester. The number of hours per semester sums up to 15, amounting to 75 clinical hours during the entire study programme. Typically, each student visits another facility every semester, completing clinical practice in five different places, with different populations (although there are exceptions, and some students stay in the same facility for a whole year). The options that are offered include: private practices for children with developmental problems, special education (including integration/inclusion programmes and segregated classes), foster care, community homes for adults with psychiatric problems, nursing homes, cardiology and rehabilitation units in hospital. Clinical hours usually start with observing, followed with co-leading, and ultimately leading the sessions under supervision.

On MA level, students are responsible for finding the placement for their practice themselves. During the studies they need to conduct at least 135 clinical hours and submit reports on their work to the academic supervisor. There is no obligatory supervisor during the practice (as these students, holding BA in MT, are qualified professionals), and group supervision is provided at school.

The equivalency programme requires 60 clinical hours under supervision in the field and group supervision at school (5 hours per semester). Students are offered a list of institutions providing music therapy services and can choose the place and population that suits their needs best.

5. Musical training

Considering the fact that the courses being described are offered at the music academy, musical training is intense, especially on the BA level. It seems important that the future music therapists not only dispose of the relevant therapeutic tools, but also are competent musicians. Also, as music therapy students in Katowice study at the music education department, they receive knowledge that enables them to teach music in public schools.

Using music therapeutically is a multidimensional skill that needs to be mastered by practice; the necessary starting point is having more than basic musical ability and awareness. As mentioned before, students who start the programme usually have decent abilities in theoretical and practical aspects of music, therefore during the studies the content of the classes is quite advanced. The obligatory music courses and numbers of hours are listed in the overview section. Thanks to aural training and harmony, at the end of the programme the students are usually able to provide harmonic accompaniment to songs without preparation, match clients pitches and harmonize or modulate during the improvisation. Receiving individual piano lessons and guitar and voice in small groups (3-6 persons), they gain instrumental and vocal skills, which makes them able to perform pieces in all styles, from classical music to current pop trends, accompany individual and group performances and facilitate music therapy sessions with aesthetic qualities. Moreover, specific course on piano improvisation is profiled in such a way that it focuses on skills needed for music therapy specifically. Orchestration classes give the students competences to arrange music in different genres for typical and non-typical sets of instruments, from string quartet to little percussion. Conducting provides the knowledge and practical applications of leading the group musically. These musical abilities, built during the courses mentioned, are at the same time put in the therapeutic context in music therapy techniques and clinical applications of music therapy classes, therefore students can use the skills they learned during music courses in the active, role-playing-based music therapy classes.

The music abilities that students are supposed to gain on BA level are:
- to play instruments (at least piano and guitar) and sing well enough to perform wide music repertoire and improvise in different styles, with application of music therapy improvisatory skills (Wigram, 2004), and adapt to specific music therapy situations,
- to orchestrate music of different styles,
- to listen to client's music in aesthetic categories (Aigen, 2007, 2008; Verney & Ansdell, 2010),
- to choose proper repertoire for receptive experiences.

These skills sum up to the ability of providing musical structures for improvising, re-creating, composing and listening experiences that are core to music therapy processes (Bruscia, 1998).

On MA level students are competent musicians and therapists, therefore only few more advanced music classes are added. Composition and arrangement is a practical course that nurtures creativity and allows for further exploring of the artistic personalities of the students. Music pedagogy and psychology of music are more theoretical and provide better understanding of processes linked to learning music and musical activities on different levels: from neuroscientific research to philosophical and psychological concepts.

Students of equivalency courses are expected to have decent music skills; they are also obliged to put in a lot of individual, home-based work into the studies. Therefore, only three courses are focused on typically musical skills: voice, improvisation in music therapy and Orff-workshops. However, during all music therapy classes, the musical abilities of students are being trained and expanded, together with practical information on how to use their skills in therapeutic context. The exercises and homework usually involve gaining musical competences that are later tested during classes and exams.

6. Experiential learning, music therapy self-experience

There are no separate classes regarding music therapy self-experience, however at all levels of studies students participate in a lot of activities that fit into experiential learning label. Most of the content of classes such as music therapy techniques, clinical applications of music therapy, improvisation, psychotherapy, art and drama therapy is covered through experiencing and reflecting on different therapeutic interventions. Usually, students try new activities or structures on themselves, then the experiences are processed verbally (or sometimes artistically, with a different artistic medium used). Role-playing is also frequently used technique that facilitates learning of future real life challenges.

In terms of typical music therapy self-experience, on the BA level, one of the semesters in music therapy techniques is entirely dedicated to therapeutic group work, with students being in the role of the clients (no grades are awarded), and – at the end – they are offered an opportunity to lead one of the sessions.

7. Evaluation procedures concerning quality of teaching

Music therapy BA and MA programmes are subject to the same rules as all the specialisations offered by The Karol Szymanowski Academy of Music. It means that at the end of each academic year students evaluate all classes they took during that time. The main part of the evaluation is based on Likert scale (students assess, for example, teacher's way of presenting, usefulness of content, punctuality, etc. from 0 – very low, to 5 – very high). Students are also encouraged to provide additional comments. It is anonymous and voluntary.

Additionally, all music therapy faculty and students meet right after the finals of the second semester just to openly discuss any issues that students raise, taking into consideration their suggestions in planning the following year. The specific feedback that the teachers get this way seems to be more beneficial. However, it is possible that providing critical comments publicly as well as personal discussions might pose some risk and bring bias into further teacher/students relationship.

Equivalency students are encouraged to send their comments and suggestions by email after each semester.

8. PhD Programme

There is no PhD programme focused specifically on music therapy at the Academy.

9. References

Aigen, K. (2007). In defense of beauty: A role for the aesthetic in music therapy theory: Part I: The development of aesthetic theory in music therapy. *Nordic Journal of Music Therapy 16*(2), 112-128.

Aigen, K. (2008). In defense of beauty: A role for the aesthetic in music therapy theory: Part II: Challenges to aesthetic theory in music therapy: Summary and response. *Nordic Journal of Music Therapy 17*(1), 3-18.

Bruscia, K. (1998). *Defining music therapy*. Gilsum, NH: Barcelona Publishers.

Verney, R., & Ansdell, G. (2010). *Conversations on Nordoff-Robbins Music Therapy*. Gilsum, NH: Barcelona Publishers.

Wigram, T. (2004). *Improvisation: Methods and techniques for music therapy clinicians, educators and students*. London: Jessica Kingsley.

11   Barcelona, Spain

Melissa Mercadal-Brotons

©Photo courtesy of Esmuc

©Photo courtesy of "L'Auditori"

MA Music Therapy Programme
Escola Superior de Música de Catalunya (ESMUC), Barcelona
http://www.esmuc.cat/eng/Master-s-Programs/Courses-offered/
Masters-Degree-in-Music-Therapy

Part-time Two-Year MA Music Therapy Programme

Escola Superior de Música de Catalunya (ESMUC), Barcelona, Catalonia, ESP

FACT SHEET

Institution:	Escola Superior de Música de Catalunya (ESMUC), Barcelona, Catalonia, Spain
Programme Head:	Dr. Melissa Mercadal-Brotons
Study Period:	4 semesters
ECTS Credits:	60
Number of students:	Max. 15 per study group
Teaching personnel capacities:	C3-Professorship (FTE), 5 W2- Professorship (0.25 FTE), 5 Adjunt faculty, Secretary (0.5 FTE), Lectureships (11).
Tuition Fee:	5,750 € (in total)
Target Group/ Addressees:	People with qualifications or a degree in Education, Speech therapy, Social Education, Nursing, Occupational therapy, Physical therapy, Psychology, Music, Medicine, Nursing. Other professionals working with people with disabilities and/or at risk of social exclusion.
Admission Requirements:	BA or an equivalent degree, practical musical skills (if the candidate does not have a music degree), ability to read and understand the English language.
Language of Instr.:	Catalan, Spanish, English
Type:	Part-time 2-year programme leading to a Master's Degree
Academic Degree:	Master of Music Therapy (M.M.T.)
Occupational Title:	Music Therapist

The following link provides further information: http://www.esmuc.cat/eng/Master-s-Programs/Courses-offered/Masters-Degree-in-Music-Therapy

1. Background: Developments, theories, and philosophy

This Master programme is based on the assumption that a music therapist is a *person* and a *professional* closely involved in music, who is committed to using it for therapeutic purposes within a helping relationship with those people who have some kind of difficulty or need for special support.

Mateos-Hernández (2011) defines a music therapist as:

> A professional with a knowledge of and an identity in both music and the therapeutic area. This professional integrates all his/her competencies through the discipline of Music therapy, to establish a relationship of socio-emotional support through musical activities in a suitable frame in order to promote and / or restore the health of people with whom he/she works, meeting their physical, emotional, mental, social and cognitive needs, and promoting significant changes in them. (p. 110)

Furthermore, this author elaborates on the underlying values of music therapists:

Constantly opt for self-knowledge, trying to make sense of their existence from a viewpoint of vital optimism, searching for truth and personal freedom, with an orientation to pro-social behaviour.

Abide by the music therapist code of ethics in everything they do.

Opt for change and continuous improvement: for themselves, the people working in the institutions and for society in general.

The music therapist is an agent of mental health in the community.

The music therapist is a didactic agent of music therapy, wherever appropriate, and is careful about how it is transmitted. (p. 111).

The learning process of students in this Master programme will lead to a preparation which should ensure their professional competence to provide a variety of learning and therapeutic experiences for their clients. In addition, students are encouraged by current research to seek, evaluate, and appropriately implement current ideas and developments in the therapeutic applications of music. This, together with the enhancement and optimization of their personal development, ensures that the future professionals value knowledge, develop intellectual curiosity, and acquire the methodological rigour and attitude of constant self-improvement, which are key to the development of the profession, both in clinical practice and research. The learning process and personal development are continuous throughout life. The personal development of the music therapist should also ensure that the future professional is sensitive to aesthetic qualities in music and life, consistently maximizing client opportunities and accomplishments, and minimizing self-aggrandizement.

2. Admission criteria and admission procedures

- A Bachelor's degree from Spain
- A qualification issued by a higher education institution belonging to the European Space for Higher Education which authorizes access to a Master's degree in the issuing country
- A qualification from a system outside the European Space for Higher Education. Although official recognition of the qualification is not necessary, applicants will need to show that the qualification accredits an equivalent level of study
- Entry to the Master by this route will not confer approval of the previous qualification or its recognition for any other purposes. Access to the Master without prior official recognition of qualifications will require the following documents:
  - Completion of the application form
  - A certified copy of the university degree, Bachelor's degree in music or equivalent, translated and legalized through diplomatic channels (LANGUAGES: Catalan, Spanish, and English)
  - A certified copy of the certificate of the subjects studied, translated and legalized through diplomatic channels

Other requirements include:
- Ability to read and understand English
- Practical music skills (if the candidate has no music qualification)
- Letter of motivation to enter the programme
- An interview (in person, or online)

Explanations:

The curricular circumstances of the concept of a part-time Master programme, for which the students have already earned a previous degree and are generally professionally active, are justified by:
- Life and professional experience of the participants
- Professionals who are active in their respective field
- Possibility of a change of primary occupation to music therapy
- Students traveling from other parts of the country to attend classes.
- Trans-regional distribution of internships and training therapy (by having students organise these themselves, e.g. close to their homes)

The different artistic and scientific experiences of the members of the heterogeneous group are integrated into the course of studies. These complement each other and at the same time allow for specialisations. Self-experience and practicum help the candidates verify their own motivation through self-reflection in a therapeutic setting and the encounter of clinical situations.

The musical part of the admission requirements determines whether the applicant is apt for the musical training in the Masters programme. Musicality and an identity as a musician or as someone who makes music are necessary. One should have a special relationship with an instrument, preferably piano, guitar or voice. It is not musical excellence that is relevant, but openness to improvise on several instruments and to play a variety of music styles which are encountered by music therapists and amongst the preferences of patients.

Since classes are taught in one of the three languages, Catalan, Spanish and/or English, students whose native language is not Catalan or Spanish must provide evidence of proficiency in the English language. The audit committee will decide on individual cases.

3. Structure and content of the curriculum

The training received through this programme, which complies with international standards, is designed to allow application of music therapeutic competence into appropriate fields, but also serves as a qualification to introduce music therapy work in new, potentially suitable institutions. The programme at Esmuc follows the standard of the European Space of Higher Education (Bologna Plan) and is oriented towards EMTC (European Music Therapy Confederation) recommendations for the European music therapy register (EMTR).

Moreover, further emphases are laid on the scientific qualifications of graduates in order to further establish quality management in music therapy through primary, application-oriented research. The Master programme is strongly linked to our research group "research and music creation" and its activities.

Overview of the structure of the programme

The programme is designed to be a two-year (4 semester), part-time, postgraduate programme, which meets every weekend (Friday and Saturday) from October to June. A total of 600 contact hours are spread over the two years:

Course contents

As can be seen in the following overview of the modules and subjects, the programme provides knowledge and skills in significant artistic and scientific areas for the future music therapist:

- Knowledge of psychology of music as a basis for music therapy interventions
- Training in practical music skills for clinical work
- Knowledge and practice of active and receptive music therapy approaches

- Fundamental knowledge in various theoretical and methodological approaches that are used internationally
- Basic psychological and psychotherapeutic knowledge
- Self-experience and self-reflective skills, individually and in group
- Current research and research methods in music therapy
- Music therapy practicum in typical music therapy areas

This training programme, therefore, integrates the following elements:
- Artistic and psychological self-experience
- Specific instrumental and vocal development
- Role-play and group dynamics
- Insight into the practical work, its documentation, reflection, and research
- Music therapy research and relevant research from health and educational allied disciplines

Here is an overview of the seven modules the program includes with the specific subjects within each module:

	ECTS	CH	SP	WL
M1 Theoretical, and scientific foundations				
Introduction to Music therapy	3	30	45	75
Psychology of Music	2	20	30	50
Introduction to research in Music Therapy	3	30	45	75
Total	8	80	120	200
M2 Applied Music Skills				
Piano playing	4	40	60	100
Guitarplaying	4	40	60	100
Voice	2	20	30	50
Ensambles and arrangements I	1	10	15	25
Ensambles and arrangements II	2	20	30	50
Improvisation and Composition	4	40	60	100
Music technology	1	10	15	25
Total	18	180	270	450
M3 Self-experience (including self-reflection)	4	80	20	100
M4 Clinical Music Therapy				
Music therapy methods	4	80	20	100
Music therapy models	1	15	10	25

	ECTS	CH	SP	WL
Music and Relaxation techniques	1	10	15	25
Total	6	105	45	150
M5 Foundations of Psychotherapy				
Abnormal Psychology	2	30	20	50
Counselling skills	2	20	30	50
Psychotherapies	4	40	60	100
Total	8	90	110	200
M6 Music Therapy Practicum				
Practicum I	2	40	10	50
Practicum II	8	150	50	200
Total	10	190	60	250
M7 Master's thesis and Presentation	6	40	110	150
Total ECTS	60			

CH (contact hours): attendance to classes and lectures; SP: expected time for preparation and follow-up; WL (workload): total workload; ECTS (credit points): European Credit Transfer System

4. Clinical training, internships

The *practicum* includes a total of 250 hours, which are structured as:

- 50 hours of institution visits, participation in team meetings, meeting potential clients, preparation and reflection with the internship instructor and supervisor.
- 100 hours of work with patients (alone and in groups)
- 30 hours of external single supervision
- 70 hours of preparation, reworking, and documentation

Practical experience for students in the field of music therapy is crucial for the Master to be viable and effective. The Practicum is a module aimed at professionalizing the student, and consists of putting into practice the clinical role of a music therapist, under the supervision of an experienced professional, and documented in a practicum report. This requires the development of professional qualities, which are essential when working in a multidisciplinary clinical context. It is therefore an experience in the use and application of knowledge acquired in classes.

The practicum is organized in two specific periods. The first period (which takes place in the first and second semesters) includes observation and active participation with professional music therapists. In the second period (which takes place in the third and fourth semesters) the student formulates and implements an intervention project in an institution with the mentoring and supervision of a professional music therapist, as a step prior to professional practice. Supervision sessions are given both through individual tutorials and in group tutorials through seminars led by active music therapists who teach in the programme. Students are welcome to do their practicum in a wide variety of centres and community settings in the areas of Education, Mental Health, Medicine, Community, and Geriatric care.

5. Musical training

The content of the musical training is based on fundamental music therapy approaches (Darrow, 2004). This is valid for both the practical and the theoretical competences. In order to accomplish the musical techniques within the music therapy situations, it is necessary to complete a specific training that includes exercises at home. Requirements are musicality, identity as a musician, openness to improvisation, as well as specific functional musical skills in piano, guitar, and voice.

Music skills include:

The ability to play accompanying instruments, voice control, improvisation, ability to lead ensembles, composition, musical arrangements, knowledge of a variety of repertoire and musical styles, etc., along with teaching techniques related to music education. These skills enable the music to be adapted to the different levels of the participants.

Specific competencies addressed include the following:

- Development of useful musical skills to work in music therapy sessions
- Creation of own musical resources for specific objectives
- Mastery of a first musical instrument to improvise in different situations with ease
- Acquisition of basic skills on a second musical instrument as a reference tool for intervention
- Development of a high level of sensitivity and flexibility in the practice of music therapy
- Analysis of the unconventional musical language, understanding its relation to elements linked to inter-subjective processes and non-verbal communication.

The musical competences that are to be acquired, primarily follow the repertoire of active and receptive music therapy approaches. These are:

- Music playing live, or where appropriate, recorded
- Singing songs for/ with the patient
- Free, theme or rule-oriented improvisation (vocal or instrumental)
- Musical role-play

The therapeutic relationship in music therapy is mainly developed on a musical level and needs musical relationship skills – the skill to communicate through music. Examples include playing for the patient, empathic accompaniment of songs, improvised dialogue, or group improvisation. The music therapy relationship develops with the help of a repertoire of music-oriented approaches that, modified according to the specific process, are offered to the patients.

The competences are taught in class through

- Improvising, musically free and with guidelines like bourdon or cadence structures
- Improvising and expressing oneself through body movement
- Vocal and song related competences (quality of the voice, song repertoire, spontaneous singing and instrumental accompaniment of songs. Students are also introduced to other voice techniques such as overtone singing)
- Multi-instrumental expressiveness
- Technical/functional competences on piano and guitar (song accompaniment) as important therapeutic instruments
- Playing of rhythmic instruments
- Arranging for and playing in different ensembles, which may include traditional acoustic instruments, electric instruments, Orff instruments.

The student is offered a variety of specific practical music learning experiences, for example in the form of solos, duos or group playing, group exercises and role-play, or experimental music activities. Feedback from the group is a good way to develop or discover implicit and intuitive understanding of possible meanings of non-verbal, acoustic expressive, and interactive behaviour.

In order to use songs in music therapy, one needs to acquire repertoire, knowledge of how to perform, arrange, and possibly rehearse songs from different times and of different styles. One should be able to accompany simple songs as a way of responding to the patient. The combination of songs, dance, and playing is important for the practical work in various clinical areas.

Training and use of the voice as the instrument closest to the body is important for spontaneity with patients using the vocal improvisation of songs. Vocal training and speech training promote awareness for the handling of one's own voice. Body and breath awareness are also important for receptive music therapy. The conscious integration of the body at peace and in movement is a central therapeutic factor.

Rhythm is a key element in music therapy. Training in various pitched and non-pitched percussion instruments is therefore essential. Rhythmic competence and empathic synchronization are carrying and structuring elements in the music therapy relationship. Both the learning of playing techniques and rhythmic, improvisatory elements are practiced. Students are also introduced to drum circles and body percussion techniques.

Songs, rhythm exercises and several music therapy improvisations will be practiced and evaluated during active approaches in class and in the community under the supervision of a music therapist. Different types of improvisation techniques, using voice, instruments and dance/movement are presented and practiced in class, and students are involved in reflexions about the process of the live experiences. Later, transferences are made to clinical settings with a variety of populations. Students are encouraged to move beyond their comfort zone by trying as many different mediums as possible.

Another component of the musical training is the introduction to music and relaxation techniques. Students have the opportunity to learn about how to choose appropriate music for relaxation purposes. They are also exposed to a variety of relaxation techniques, and have the opportunity to practice some of them under the supervision of a professional music therapist trained in this technique.

Since, there is a rapidly emerging and developing area of music therapy practice that uses electronic music technologies in a range of therapeutic and clinical settings to help clients with complex needs, students learn about these technologies and their applications in clinical settings serving children and adults.

At the end of the programme, graduates are able to offer and carry out a variety of music techniques, both active and receptive, confidently and competently.

6. Experiential learning, music therapy self-experience

Being a music therapist requires a high level of sensitivity and flexibility, which relies on reflective relation skills. According to Bruscia (2014), "Self-experience is an umbrella term for a wide range of pedagogical practices used in the education, training, and supervision of music therapists. By definition, self-experiences involve both active engagement in the learning process and some form of self-inquiry. In this context, active engagement means that the learner participates in the practice of music therapy, either in the role of client or therapist, and by so doing, learns how to manage respective processes" (p. 16).

Self-experience is an integral part of our curriculum. The programme in Esmuc includes 100 hours of group therapy and individual supervision training. The aim of supervision is to work on professional and personal development both with regard to the patient and to music therapy techniques. The group therapy is integrated into teaching blocks, while the individual supervision training is done outside the classroom during the master programme. Both components are conducted by professional music therapists.

7. Evaluation procedures concerning quality of teaching

In the academic year 2015-2016 the programme will be offered in Esmuc, an institution of higher education in music, for the first time. However, the programme started in 2001 and has moved to different locations. From 2001 to 2014, the programme was evaluated by the different institutions like any other master's programme. The evaluations focused on each of the subjects, their professors-lecturers, as well as the coordination and leadership of the programme. During the evaluation, students are encouraged to give constructive criticism in terms of desires and suggestions for changes.

8. Continuing Education/Professional Development

In addition to the master program, ESMUC also offers courses and workshops for professional music therapists interested in furthering their professional development.

9. References

Bruscia, K. (2014). *Self-experiences in music therapy education, training and supervision.* Gilsum, NH: Barcelona Publishers

Darrow, A.A. (Ed.). (2004). Introduction to approaches in music therapy. Silver Spring, MD: The American Music Therapy Association.

Mateos-Hernández, L.A. (2011). Fundamentos en Musicoterapia [Fundamentals of music therapy]. In L.A. Mateos-Hernández (Ed.), *Terapias Artístico Creativas* [Creative arts therapies] (pp. 105-144). Salamanca: Amarú.

Internet sources:

Asociación Española de Musicoterapeutas Profesionales (AEMP). (2008). *Documento Técnico Recomendaciones orientativas para valorar la calidad de un postgrado universitario de musicoterapia en España,* 2008. Retrieved from http://media.wix.com/ugd/643546_c042420329814b7c817eeff67a103769.pdf.

Asociación Española de Musicoterapeutas Profesionales (AEMP). (2011). *Código Ético para los Musicoterapeutas Profesionales en España,* 2011. Retrieved from http://media.wix.com/ugd/643546_0884a74137164614b3459437ef0a301d.pdf.

Asociaciones Españolas de musicoterapia afiliadas a la EMTC (AEMTA-EMTC). (2014). Código Ético de la Musicoterapia en España. *Sintoní@ Digital. Boletín-Revista de Musicoterapia,* 52, 5-9.

European Music Therapy Confederation. (2015). *Training courses.* Retrieved from http://emtc-eu.com/courses/.

Further recommended readings:

Bruscia, K. (1989). *Defining Music Therapy*. Gilsum, NH: Barcelona Publishers.

Goodman, K.D. (Ed.). (2015). *International perspectives in music therapy education and training*. Springfield, IL: Charles C Thomas.

Mercadal-Brotons, M., & Mateos Hernández, L. A. (2005). Contributions towards the consolidation of music therapy in Spain within the European Space for Higher Education (ESHE). *Music Therapy Today, 6* (4). Retrieved from: http://www.wfmt.info/ Musictherapyworld/modules/archive/stuff/reports/Proceedings_Screen.pdf#page=25

Mercadal-Brotons, M., Sabbatella, P. L., & Del Moral Marcos, M. T. (2015). Spain. Country report on professional recognition of music therapy. *Approaches: Music Therapy & Special Music Education, Special Issue 7*(1), 181–182.

Sabbatella, P. (2005). Music Therapy Training within the European Higher Education System: A Survey on Music Therapy Training Courses in Spain. In D. Aldridge, J. Fachner, & J. Erkkilä (Eds.), Many Faces of Music Therapy – Proceedings of the 6th European Music Therapy Congress, June 16–20, 2004 Jyväskylä, Finland. *Music Therapy Today, 6* (4). Retrieved from: http://www.wfmt.info/Musictherapyworld/modules/ archive/stuff/reports/Proceedings_Screen.pdf#page=25

Wheeler, B.L. (2015). *Music therapy handbook*. New York, NY: Guilford.

12   Roehampton, London, UK

Tessa Watson

Photo: Courtesy of University of Roehampton, London

Photo: Courtesy of University of Roehampton, London

MA Music Therapy Programme
University of Roehampton, London
http://www.roehampton.ac.uk/postgraduate-courses/music-therapy/index.html

Full and part-time MA Music Therapy Programme
University of Roehampton, London, GBR

FACT SHEET

Institution:	University of Roehampton, London, United Kingdom Whitelands College
Programme Head:	Tessa Watson
Study Period:	2 years (full time), 4 years (part time)
ECTS Credits:	120
Number of students:	Max. 12 per study group (8 full time, 4 part time)
Teaching personnel capacities:	Course Convenor (0.4 FTE), 3 Senior Lecturers (0.6 FTE) administrator, other staff from the Psychology Department and specialist visiting lecturers
Tuition Fees:	£545 per 10 credits, £13,080 for the whole training (home students);
	£725 per 10 credits, £17,400 (international students)
Target Group/ Addressees:	There is no specific target group of people who might be suitable for the training, however, admission requirements are given below.
Adm. Requirements:	Usually an honours degree (though see later section on admission requirements), a high standard of musical skills, work experience with one or more of the client groups with whom Music Therapists work, psychological mindedness and readiness to work at Master's level.
Language of Instr.:	English
Type:	Full time or Part-time Programme (Master's Degree)
Academic Degree:	Master of Arts (MA)
Occupational Title:	Music Therapist
Others:	PhD Programme (see p. 150)

University of Roehampton, Erasmus House, Roehampton Lane, London SW15 5PU, UK.

1. Background: Developments, theories, and philosophy

Music therapy in the UK

This course provides a professional training in music therapy, approved by the Health and Care Professions Council in the UK. Music therapy aims to help individuals to develop skills and self-understanding through a primarily non-verbal relationship in music. Through the use of music the therapist facilitates the individual's move towards increased well-being in the form of specific therapeutic aims. Music therapy as practised in the UK is largely based on improvisation – the music being the shared, spontaneous creation of client and therapist. Other styles of music, including song writing, the use of technology and pre-composed music are also used as appropriate to the need of the individual.

In the UK, music therapists work within a wide range of clinical settings. They work with people of all ages; from infants and young children through to elderly adults. Music therapists work within statutory services (such as the National Health Service (NHS), education or social services), within charities and private organisations, and in private practice. Music therapy can benefit people with a wide range of difficulties or challenges, including mental health problems, learning disabilities and autism, dementia and neurology, as well as people experiencing serious illness such as cancer or those who have experienced trauma. Music therapists often work as part of a multi-disciplinary team, and frequently work in partnership with other disciplines (Twyford & Watson, 2008).

Theoretical stance of the Roehampton training

The emphasis of the training at Roehampton is on the relationship, primarily considered through a psychoanalytic framework; Sobey and Woodcock write that 'this does not detract from the value of the music which has a vital role to play in creating opportunities for shared experiences and increasing their significance.' (1999, p. 133). In their chapter, which describes the Roehampton training and approach, they refer to John who suggests that 'the clue to the meaning is not hidden somewhere in the music but in the shared experience of client and therapist' (1994, p. 160). In order to support students in their development as psychodynamic practitioners, different areas of theory and practice are studied in depth. Psychoanalytic theories such as the unconscious and defences, attachment (Bowlby, 2005; Howe 2011), containment (Bion, 1962), affect attunement (Stern, 1985), and secondary handicap (Sinason, 1986) are read and discussed. Ideas about relationship, including transference and countertransference, and boundaries are introduced.

There is study of Winnicott's theories and Klein's theory of object relations (Winnicott, 1990, 2001 and Levinge, 2015; Klein, 1997). Groups and group dynamics are considered (Bion, 1961). Trainees also think about the role and qualities of a therapist, studying some aspects of Rogers' works (1967) and reading research into therapist efficacy. Additional teaching by specialist lecturers gives a thorough understanding of child development, and of different conceptualisations of mental health, learning disability and autism (Watson, 2007). All these theories are undertaken with reference to music therapy practice and examples which focus on the techniques, processes and effects of music therapy.

Observational studies

Early in the training a ten week infant observation is undertaken. Students observe a primary care giver (usually a mother) and infant in the home setting for ten one-hour periods. The observation is discussed in a weekly series of seminars which focus upon a psychoanalytic interpretation of observed events. This gives students the opportunity to study psychoanalytical concepts further from this particular perspective, consider the establishment of a first relationship, think in detail about non-verbal interaction and to consider music therapy in this area (Edwards, 2011). Importantly this observation also awakens in the trainee therapist the ability to take a neutral role, and to observe in detail all those present (including the trainee themselves). Bick writes 'students learn to watch and feel before jumping in with theories' (1987, p. 254). Students are encouraged to develop their abilities to receive and think about difficult feelings, rather than acting in order to dispel their own discomfort. The infant observation provides a starting point for understanding and performing containment as therapist (Bion, 1959). In addition, it brings to life other psychoanalytical theories, such as object relations (Klein), transference and counter-transference.

As trainees develop their own identity as music therapists, they are encouraged to reflect on the history of the music therapy profession in the UK (Barrington, 2015; Darnley-Smith & Patey, 2001) and to explore literature and theories that may be broader than those at the heart of the training, in order that they can develop a therapeutic practice that is congruent with their own personal stance. Broad reading is encouraged. Different clinical areas will demand different approaches and the Roehampton training equips trainees with a coherent framework that can be adapted for use within broad clinical areas.

The last modules of the training are designed to provide students with an introduction to the research process and to research methodologies used in music therapy and arts therapies research. The modules will enable students to understand and critically evaluate several different methodologies and to undertake a small research project (Wheeler, 2005). This research project enables the student to experience the research process, complete a small research project and thus take research skills into their future workplace.

See below for detail of the music modules, personal therapy and placement modules.

2. Admission criteria and admission procedures

The programme may be studied full-time (4 semesters/2 academic years) or part time (8 semesters/4 academic years, or 6 semesters/3 academic years. The programme is designed to train musicians as therapists with the ability and flexibility to practise professionally with a wide range of clients within the NHS, education, social services or private sector. Since it is the MA which confers the professional qualification it is necessary to complete successfully all the modules pertaining to that section of the programme with a total of 240 credits at level 7 (120 ETCS credits).

The MA Music Therapy programme at University of Roehampton is intended to enable competent, practising musicians to train as therapists, bringing together their skills, education and other life experiences in the service of some of the most disadvantaged members of the community. It therefore has special appeal for mature musicians and other professionals with the requisite musical ability who wish to make a career change. Students are expected to be able to demonstrate their ability to follow a postgraduate programme, and to have had some experience with the kinds of client most often referred for music therapy.

Admission requirements:

- An honours degree, usually in music. Other subjects are considered where music skills are demonstrably sufficient. Consideration is given to mature students without a degree who may have professional qualifications or work and life experience which is relevant and useful.

- A professional standard of proficiency on an instrument or voice, together with some keyboard skills where piano is not the first study.

- The potential to use musical skills in professional music therapy practice and the ability to communicate musically.

- Maturity of personality and self-awareness compatible with training as a therapist.

- Two years work experience following graduation is recommended.

- Some experience of working within a setting and with clients relevant to the programme (e.g., children, adults or older adults with severe learning disabilities and autism or mental health problems).

- Evidence of a good command of written and spoken English (international students must have scores of 6.5 on IELTS tests).

- All applicants are required to supply the names of two referees. References are always taken up prior to offering a place.

- In addition to these requirements students must be prepared to enter mandatory individual personal therapy for one year of the training (paid for by the student in addition to the course fees). Students are made aware that role play (as both client and therapist) is an important learning and teaching method on the training, and they are asked to give their agreement to take part in this. Students must also be prepared to allow tutors to contact their GP or other medical doctor prior to, or during the course of the training should this be necessary. Students must also be prepared to apply and pay for enhanced Disclosure and Barring Service check (http://www.homeoffice.gov.uk/agencies-public-bodies/dbs/). These requirements link to the need to ensure students' fitness to practice at all times during the training.

- Initial selection is made through submission of application form and CD demonstrating musical performance and improvisation. A short essay on applicants' motives for entering the profession is required.

- At interview, the applicant is required to perform on their first study instrument, piano (if not first study), and voice. Some improvisation is also required at interview. The interview process is designed to engage applicants in discussion about key themes and aspects of the process of training. Applicants should come prepared to discuss their reading about music therapy in the UK.

3. Structure and content of the curriculum

FULL TIME		
Year 1		
APT020L001Y	Theory I: Human Development and Growth	Compulsory
MUT040L220A	Music therapy theory and practice 1 and 2	Compulsory
MUT020L223Y	Observational studies	Compulsory
MUT020L224Y	Music studies; clinical improvisation	Compulsory
MUT020L225S	Music studies; repertoire	Compulsory
MUT020L226Y	Music therapy placement 1	Compulsory
Year 2		
MUT020L227Y	Music therapy placement 2	Compulsory
APT020L002Y	Process Group and Personal Formulation	Compulsory
APT020L007A	Research Methods	Compulsory
APT040L008Y	Research Portfolio	Compulsory

For more detail of these modules please see our webpage at: http://www.roehampton.ac.uk/postgraduate-courses/music-therapy/index.html

The MA aims to:

1. provide students with a thorough and systematic knowledge, experience, skills and confidence to work as a professionally qualified music therapist so that they can demonstrate a comprehensive understanding of therapeutic techniques and approaches as required for professional registration purposes;

2. provide students with a thorough in depth and systematic understanding, from specific theoretical perspectives, for the practice of music therapy while relating these to treatment models in other appropriate forms of psychological therapy or other forms of treatment;

3. give students an understanding of clients' conditions and experience by means of clinical studies in related disciplines, for example infant psychology, psychiatry, psychoanalysis, and the user's experience.

4. extend students' musical skills and facilitate an understanding of how these can be used to meet the therapeutic needs of clients.

5. provide students with appropriate clinical placements, with adequate supervision, in order to develop their capacity to work confidently, effectively and professionally in complex organisations with challenging client populations;

6. develop the student's ability to critically assess and reflect upon their role as potential reflective professional practitioners by active exploration and critical analysis of the key processes involved in therapeutic work and relationships;

7. provide opportunities for students to reflect and focus on their self-development, self-awareness, interpersonal sensitivities and creativity as they develop their identity as autonomous and creative therapists;

8. provide students with a thorough and comprehensive understanding of appropriate policy, legal and ethical issues, including equal opportunity and diversity issues related to therapeutic practice so that they can demonstrate an awareness and ability to manage the implications of complex ethical dilemmas, work pro-actively with others in the formulation and implementation of solutions and apply this understanding to complex and unpredictable situations;

9. develop student skills in the critical evaluation of appropriate research, in respect to a wide range of diagnostic groups in order that their eventual therapeutic practice is evidence based. In addition to provide students with the opportunity to critically evaluate and examine, at masters level, a range of research methodologies appropriate to the arts therapies in general and, where appropriate, to conduct a research project as part of their final year project work.

The programme aims to encourage a questioning critical and evaluative approach to both theory and practice. There is a balance between experiential learning and rigorous academic study at an advanced level. The course emphasises the emotional development of the student practitioner together with clinical exploration through critical enquiry.

4. Clinical training, internships

Placements lie at the heart of the music therapy programme. In working with their own individual client and group, students have the opportunity to establish a significant therapeutic relationship with clients and engage in a process that is potentially beneficial for all those involved. With sufficient supervision provided within the programme and the opportunity to share in the experiences of those students working in different settings, students are prepared for future work as professional therapists.

In the Autumn semester students visit a range of work settings and meet with music therapists employed there. These experiences are discussed in weekly seminars and form part of placement preparation. Placement 1 is from January – June in the first year (second year for part time students), and Placement 2 from September – March of the second year (third/fourth year for part time students). In each placement students spend one day a week in the setting. They work with either one individual or one group, and usually also work as co-therapist for a fellow student, for approximately six months, an average of twenty sessions. Groupwork is given particular emphasis as music therapists in the UK are expected to run groups as part of their caseload (Davies, Richards & Barwick, 2014). Students may also take part in clinical work with their placement manager, and take on their own additional clinical work if appropriate. As well as contact time with clients, the placement day is likely to comprise of the student attending some of the following; clinical meetings, supervision, assessment sessions, and undertaking clinical note keeping. A placement manager (usually a music therapist) makes the practical arrangements, provides on-site advice and support and liaises with University supervisors. Supervision on each case takes place at University in groups. These one or two-hour groups enable students to benefit from not only presenting their clinical work (approximately once every 3 weeks) but also to follow in detail the work of their colleagues in different work settings. If students so wish, they may be able to take on additional clinical work following completion of their second placement.

In supervision, students orally present their sessions, assisted by their own detailed practice notes together with audio/video recordings where possible. Thus they learn to describe their work in detail and analyse their own techniques. Self-reflection is integral to the supervision process and thus students become aware of how their own process plays its part in the therapeutic relationship. They are encouraged to become more aware of the impact of the work environment and of the staff and institutional dynamics on clients and on the therapeutic relationship. Placement managers assist students to communicate within a multi-disciplinary team and to acquire skills in report writing.

Students are expected to conduct themselves in a professional manner at all times and adhere to the Code of Ethics and Conduct of British Association for Music Therapy as well as Health and Care Professions Council Guidance on conduct and ethics for students. Students are required to pass the first placement before being allowed to progress into the next year of the programme.

5. Musical training

Clinical improvisation is designed to help the student explore and extend the technical, expressive and interactional aspects of his/her improvisation skills and to relate these to specific theoretical concepts. This enables them to develop appropriate modes of working to meet client needs. Studies are planned to help students apply these skills most effectively in the context of music therapy theory and practice.

Students are divided into small groups. Initially tasks are suggested to assist them in attuning to the musical and non-musical behaviour of others and expanding musical vocabulary. As progress is made in other areas of the programme it becomes possible to relate practice more specifically to theoretical concepts and to make connections between musical responses and therapeutic interventions. This is largely done through role-play.

The repertoire module gives students further opportunities to build up musical resources through workshops in percussion and voice and in repertoire group (Wigram & Baker, 2005). In this practical session, musical examples from casework are brought for problem-solving through role play. Additionally, students take on the role of leader in composition workshops, where they direct a composition using the strengths and variety of instrumentation available. Reflection on the students' own music and use of their instruments is encouraged to develop a reflective musical stance (Oldfield, Tomlinson & Loombe 2015).

Summary of syllabus:

Attuning to Clients
- Accompanying and reflecting clients' musical and non-musical behaviour
- Creating and responding to mood
- Placing clients' sounds in a musical context
- Matching rhythm and rhythmic movements
- Qualities of silence
- Ways of meeting specific musical output, e.g., obsessive and rigid playing
- Chaotic sound
- Fragmented music

Increasing repertoire
- Effects of concentrating on specific musical elements: melody, harmony, rhythm
- Familiarity and fluency within different idioms

- Limited musical material such as focusing on specific intervals, ostinati, pre-composed motifs and themes
- Use of song work and song writing
- Use of guitar in music therapy

Improvisation techniques related to therapeutic theory

- Developing musical empathy
- Affect attunement
- Containment
- Limit setting and boundaries
- Structuring and directiveness addressed in music
- Improvisation related to stages in pre-verbal communication
- Styles of leadership in groupwork
- The role of a co-therapist

6. Experiential learning, music therapy self-experience

Personal therapy is a recognised and established requisite to training as a therapist and a mandatory requirement for professional accreditation by the Health and Care Professions Council. Insight into personal and group processes is a cornerstone of clinical practice and avoids the inappropriate intrusion of the therapists' own issues into their clinical relationships. As is the case on all music therapy programmes in the UK, students are required to have experience of their own personal therapy. On the Roehampton training, students are part of a training group that runs for the duration of their first year (full time students) or second year (part time students). The group provides a consistent group experience, which is seen as an essential component in the personal and professional development of a music therapist. The group also offers the students the chance to share their experiences of all aspects of the course, and of the practice of music therapy, in a confidential setting. In addition, students must engage in individual therapy which they must fund themselves. This may be psychotherapy, or one of the HCPC registered Arts Therapies.

The student will need to show a developing capacity for self-reflexivity and awareness of their own role in the therapeutic relationship. Additionally they need to demonstrate an emotional understanding of what they have to offer the client and what areas they particularly need to address in their future work (Watson, 2005). Tutors suggest that students keep an ongoing personal log or diary relating to their experiences on this module and in their personal therapy. This will assist with the assignment related to this module and also provides a useful vehicle for reflection.

In addition, personal tutorials are arranged for each student at set intervals during the training to reflect on their overall progress through the training.

7. Evaluation procedures concerning quality of teaching

The University has an annual evaluation governance process (the Programme Annual Review) which the music therapy programme is required to complete. This includes scrutiny from colleagues, academic advisors and also detailed feedback from students.

In addition, the programme is subject to stringent approval and monitoring process from Health and Care Professions Council (the UK regulating body; http://www.hcpc-uk.co.uk/). Students who have successfully completed an approved training course are eligible to apply for HCPC registration.

8. PhD Programme

Expressions of interest are welcomed from qualified music therapists who wish to undertake research studies. Supervisory support is drawn from the Psychology Department (Arts and Play Therapies, Psychology, and Counselling and Psychotherapy) as appropriate.

9. References

Barrington, A. (2015). Perspectives on the development of the music therapy profession in the UK. *Approaches: Music Therapy & Special Music Education, Special Issue 7*(1), 118–122.

Bick, E. (1987). Notes on infant observation in psychoanalytical training. In M. Harris Williams (Ed.), *Collected Papers of Martha Harris and Esther Bick* (pp. 240–256). Perthshire: Clunie Press.

Bion, W.R. (1959). Attacks on Linking. In E. Bott Spillius (Ed.), *Melanie Klein Today: Developments in theory and practice* (Vol. 1). London: Routledge.

Bion, W. (1961). *Experiences in groups.* London: Routledge.

Bion, W. (1962). *Learning from experience.* London: Heinemann.

Bowlby, J. (2005). *The making and breaking of affectional bonds.* London: Routledge. (Original work published 1979).

Darnley-Smith, R., &Patey, H. (2001). *Music Therapy.* London: Sage.

Davies, A., Richards, E, & N. Barwick (2014). *Group music therapy. A group analytic approach.* London: Routledge.

Edwards, J. (2011). *Music Therapy and Parent-Infant Bonding.* Oxford: Oxford University Press.

Howe, D. (2011). *Attachment across the lifecourse. A brief introduction.* London: Palgrave MacMillan.

John, D. (1994). The Therapeutic Relationship in Music Therapy as a Tool in the Treatment of Psychosis In T. Wigram, B. Saperston, & R. West (Eds.), *The art and science of music therapy: A handbook* (pp. 157-166). UK: Harwood Academic.

Klein, M. (1997). Our adult world and its roots in infancy. In M. Klein, *Envy and gratitude, and other works, 1946-1963* (pp. 247-263). London: Vintage.

Levinge, A. (2015). *The Music of Being: Music Therapy, Winnicott and the School of Object Relations.* London: Jessica Kingsley.

Oldfield, A., Tomlinson, J., & Loombe, D. (2015). *Flute, Accordion or Clarinet? Using the Characteristics of our Instruments in Music Therapy.* London: Jessica Kingsley.

Rogers, C. (1967). *On becoming a person: A therapist's view of psychotherapy.* London: Constable.

Sinason, V. (1986). Secondary handicap and its relation to trauma. *Psychoanalytic Psychotherapy 2,* 131-154.

Sobey, K., & Woodcock, J. (1999). Psychodynamic Music Therapy Considerations in Training. In A. Cattanach (Ed.), *Process in the arts therapies* (pp. 132-154). London: Jessica Kingsley.

Stern, D. (1985). *The interpersonal world of the infant.* New York: Basic Books.

Twyford, K., & Watson, T. (2008). *Integrated team working. Music therapy as part of transdisciplinary and collaborative approaches.* London: Jessica Kingsley.

Watson, T. (2005). Steering a path through change. Observations on the process of training. *British Journal of Music Therapy, 19*(1) 9-15.

Watson, T. (2007). *Music therapy with adults with learning disabilities.* London: Routledge.

Wheeler, B (2005). *Music therapy research. Quantitative and qualitative perspectives* (2nd ed.). Gilsum, NH: Barcelona Publishers.

Wigram, T., & Baker, F. (2005). *Songwriting methods, techniques and clinical applications for music therapy clinicians, educators and students.* London: Jessica Kingsley.

Winnicott, D.W. (1990). The theory of the parent infant relationship. In D.W. Winnicott, *The maturational processes and the facilitating environment* (pp. 37-55). London: Karnac.

Winnicott, D.W. (2001). *Playing and reality.* UK: Bruner Routledge.

13   Conclusions: Theme and Variations

Thomas Stegemann, Hans Ulrich Schmidt, Elena Fitzthum and Tonius Timmermann

In 1970, – according to a study by Karin Schumacher, née Reissenberger (1970) – there were no more than four music therapy training courses in Europe: Vienna (Austria), Berlin (West Germany), Rostock (East Germany), and London (UK). Less than 50 years later, about 120 music therapy training courses have spread all over Europe, documenting the fascinating development and growth of an "exotic subject" somewhere between music, medicine, psychotherapy and pedagogy. In chapter 2 of this book, we have shown the "map" of European music therapy training courses, and the appendix table offers some more details about every programme. Of course, the music therapy landscape is ever changing and thus it cannot be within the scope of a book publication to provide the newest information, but a copious collection of internet links will help to find the desired information.

In addition to the vast overview of all music therapy training courses in Europe, we aimed at portraying some curricula in detail by inviting colleagues from 10 selected countries to describe their training programmes following a given structure. We tried to document the diversity and the development of European music therapy education by choosing training courses representing the three EMTC-regions (North, Middle, and South) as well as different stages of development in terms of the time that particular curriculum was established. Three sites belong to the North (Aalborg/Denmark, Liepaja/Latvia, and Roehampton/UK), four to the Middle (Vienna/Austria, Leuven/Belgium, Augsburg/Germany, and Katowice/Poland), and three to the South (Paris/France, Ferrara/Italy, and Barcelona/Spain). The "ages" of the training courses span a period of more than 56 years: the training course in Vienna was established in 1959, the training programme in Barcelona started in 2015 (for an overview see Fig. 7).

Further, different music therapy approaches are covered. We don't claim to present a representative sample – the selection is just a snapshot and a small portion of the huge European music therapy landscape. However, this selection seems to be European music therapy education in a nutshell. In the following we will summarize and comment on the topics from the subheadings of every chapter, i.e. we will analyse the "variations" with respect to the given framework which served as our "theme".

> Note: Even if we talk of specific countries in the following sections, it is important to state that there is no such thing as a 'German' or an 'Italian' or a 'Spanish music therapy'. In particular, music therapy curricula might be very different in one and the same country – thus, speaking of a distinct country usually refers to the particular training course from that country.

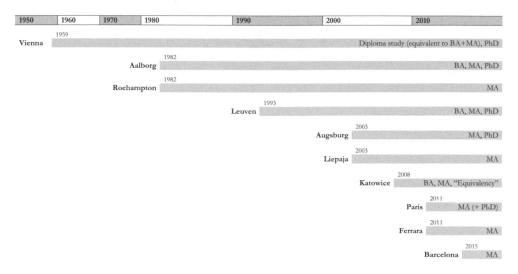

Fig. 7 Timeline and overview of ten European music therapy training courses (for details see chapter 3–12)

1. Background: Developments, theories, and philosophy

In contrast to music therapy in other areas of the world (in particular North America), it seems that in Europe the psychotherapeutic heritage is still quite dominant. In particular, in countries with a strong and rich tradition in psychodynamic psychotherapy (e.g., Austria, Belgium, France, Germany, UK) the relatedness between music therapy curricula and different psychodynamic schools (psychoanalysis, depth psychotherapy) are very pronounced and identifiable. The Italian curriculum in Ferrara is strongly influenced by developmental psychology (Stern, Trevarthen), which can be seen as a very important reference framework for modern music therapy in general. In other countries, the approach is explicitly "eclectic" (e.g., Latvia and Poland) or is referred to the "multi-paradigm situation" in international music therapy (Denmark). Of course, which theories from other disciplines are adopted, is depending on the clientele and the area where music therapy is established. In Vienna, Austria, with its longstanding tradition of music therapy in mental health care institutions (psychiatry, psychosomatics), theories and approaches were very much influenced by clinical situations, and, since the 1980s, increasingly by psychotherapy. In other countries, where music therapy is not (yet) established in hospitals or mental health care institutions, but in schools, in private practice, or in homes for children with special needs, pedagogical influences are much more coining, and thus eclectic approaches are much more common.

In addition, it seems that in some countries there are strong connections and collaborations with professionals from other arts therapies (art, drama, dance etc.) which seem to influence the way of thinking and the way of teaching music therapy. Interestingly, the humanistic philosophy seems to be a common ground for almost each of the ten training courses portrayed in this book. This encompasses a certain therapeutic stance as well as an image of the patient, rather focussing on resources, personal growth and development than on diagnoses, psychopathology, and deficits.

2. Admission criteria and admission procedures

This topic would warrant a book of its own. The main question in this context seems to be quite trivial: What does it take to become a good music therapist? Alone to define what is a good music therapist is a very difficult task, to predict who might be a good music therapist after completing the training is even harder. To our knowledge, there are no scientific data available, e.g. no longitudinal research studies that were conducted in order to determine which competences or personality traits are relevant predictors for successfully completing a music therapy training. Thus, today, there is no alternative but to rely on empirical values. Apart from differing formal criteria, which are usually prescribed by the particular institution where the music therapy training course is located, there are some communalities that can be found when comparing the admission criteria and procedures of the selected European music therapy training courses in this book.

First of all, as we are focusing on academic training programmes, a high school diploma or qualification for university entrance is required for entering at the BA level, and a Bachelor's degree or equivalent education for entering at the Master's level. All training courses' admission procedures include at least an interview with the candidates, some require a motivation letter in addition. Of course, musical skills are also a prerequisite for entering a music therapy training course. In almost all training courses a live performance is required, including singing and musical accompaniment at the very least. Most of the admission procedures also require (free) musical improvisation as part of the entrance exam. In many, but not all, cases, music theory and ear-training are also tested. The candidate's expected level of musicality differs enormously within the different training courses, for example, depending on the type of institution where the music therapy training programme is located (music university vs. other institutions).

Of course, economic aspects often also play a role regarding how many students are enrolled (i.e. if a course can come into existence), but with respect to quality assurance and patient safety it is an ethical imperative that economic reasons must not be the decisive factor in admission procedures.

3. Structure and content of the curriculum

The different structures of the curricula mirror the diversity of the European music training programmes as well as different needs and target groups. It ranges from 2-year part-time programmes with 60 ECTS credits (e.g. Barcelona) to

4-5 year full-time programmes with 240-360 ECTS (e.g. Aalborg, Leuven, Vienna). Given the diverging stages of development regarding music therapy in different countries, the various music therapy approaches and traditions, and the different educations systems, it is quite astonishing that there are a lot of commonalities regarding the contents of the ten training courses which are described in detail in this book. As we will see in the following paragraphs, there are some components of the curriculum that seem to build a common ground for a music therapy formation, including musical training, self-experience or experiential learning, and practical training in terms of internships, placements or practicums. As stated elsewhere (Timmermann et al., 2013), we have outlined six "basic module" for music therapy curricula, we consider – against the backdrop of a psychotherapy oriented understanding of music therapy – as essential: musical training, interdisciplinary scientific fundamentals, theory and practice of music therapy, basics of medicine, basics of psychotherapy, and self-experience. Interestingly, when comparing and analysing the contents of the training programmes selected for this publication, it appears that there are four "basic modules" that can be identified in each of the ten curricula:

1. music therapy core (including self-experience and internships)

2. musical and artistic formation

3. medical and psychological foundations

4. miscellaneous (e.g. writing the thesis, scientific subjects, other arts therapies)

In eight out of ten curricula it was possible to determine the amount of time (respectively the number of credits) scheduled for each of the areas/modules, and thus we could calculate the mean percentage for the modules (see Fig. 8).

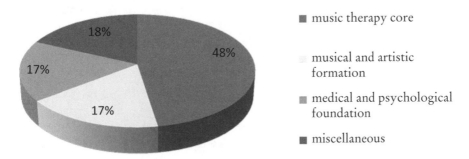

Fig. 8 Mean percentage of the four "basic modules" across eight music therapy training programmes

Not surprisingly, subjects that can be allocated to "music therapy core" build the largest part of the curricula (range: 34-57%). Interestingly, "musical and artistic formation" and "medical and psychological foundation" as well as "miscellaneous" come out more or less at the same level. Of course, the emphasis laid on the different modules differs enormously across the training programmes. For example, the percentage of "musical and artistic formation" ranges from 2 to 40%, and the proportion of "medical and psychological foundation" from 4 to 38%. These differences make clear how diverging the foci of curriculum contents in different training courses are, and how huge the variations are within different music therapy approaches alone in Europe. As stated above, this does not reflect the "quality" of a particular programme, rather it stresses the diverging needs and emphases of music therapy training in different places due to regional or national circumstances.

4. Clinical training, internships

As stated above, music therapy internships are at the heart of a music therapist's formation. This is the place where students are given the opportunity to transfer their theoretical knowledge into clinical practice, to road-test their musical and therapeutic competences and skills, and to develop their own style. This implies diligent preparation, including a thorough knowledge and skills in music therapy and fundamental knowledge of medical and psychological basics, as well as adequate onsite supervision. The structure and length of internship vary hugely within the curricula, ranging from 75 clinical hours for receiving the Bachelor's degree to 765 hours in a 4-year full-time programme. According to the criteria of the European music therapist register (EMTR), a minimum of 200 hours of documented individual supervision on music therapy clinical work is required (see: http://emtc-eu.com/register/). Although the EMTR is conceptualized as a postgraduate degree (two years of documented full time clinical experience are mandatory), it seems reasonable that a major part of clinical work's supervision should take place during the music therapy training. Further, it seems important to harmonise the amount of hours of internships with other healthcare professions (respectively other comparable professional groups) to adjust the level of professional education to that of professions that work in the same field. This might help to improve the quality of music therapy in general, and to promote the "image" and the recognition of music therapy as a still quite young profession.

What most of the training courses portrayed here do have in common is that they require individual and group therapy experiences during the internships and that they require students to work both with adults and children/adolescents in various fields. In Vienna, for example, mandatory internships encompass child and adolescent psychiatry, psychiatry, and psychosomatics. In addition, the students have to choose three practicums of the following electives: neonatology, pediatric oncology, special education, neurology, neurorehabilitation, and geriatrics.

As the areas in which music therapy is offered, are continuously expanding, one of the most challenging questions in designing music therapy curricula is, what should music therapy students be taught in practice fields, and what are they expected to teach themselves through self-learning or learning on-the-job later in their career? And further, is there a tendency that basics are taught at Bachelor's level, and that Master programmes offer a specialisation? For example, the MA training course in Würzburg-Schweinfurt, Germany focuses on music therapy in the treatment of clients with special needs (developmental disorders, rehabilitation), and of clients with dementia. At least in mental health care there is a tendency that psychotherapy schools are superseded by evidence-based and diagnosis-specific treatment models. This poses the question how music therapy curricula can manage the balancing act between offering a wide basis of music therapy methods and techniques as a starting point for further specializations, and preparing their students for specific requirements of the job market. To date, it seems that the fields of music therapy internships depend more on the people involved in the training courses and the connections to particular music therapists, institutions or hospitals that offer placements for students, than on strategic directions and evaluations concerning developments in society and research.

5. Musical training

As shown above, the percentage of "musical and artistic formation" within the curricula ranges from 2 to 40%. This is clearly not a statement of how important (or unimportant) "music" is in a particular music therapy training course. It rather shows that musical training plays a different role in the different curricula, depending on various factors. One important factor is how musical training is integrated in music therapy core subjects – thus, a low percentage in the module "musical and artistic formation" can be just an "artefact" due to the labelling of courses. Secondly, it depends on the students' prior understanding and musical skills, i.e. someone with a Bachelor's degree in music who is studying music therapy on a Master's level usually does not need to study their instrument to the same extent as a music therapy student without prior musical formation at university level. Thirdly, it depends on the institution, where a music therapy training course is located, as it may be easier to organise music lessons at a University of Music than, let us say, at a Medical University. Last but not least, it is of course an economic factor – individual music lessons or guitar practicums in small groups are much more expensive than a lecture for a huge audience.

Irrespective of the extent of "musical and artistic formation", there is no doubt about the value of musical training as part of a music therapy training programme. To quote from the chapter written by Stine Lindahl Jacobsen and Lars Ole Bonde: "The two cornerstones of the training are the development of the musical identity and the therapeutic identity and learning how to balance them" (p. 67). The aims of musical training within a music therapy curriculum are completely different from the learning objectives of an artistic study. As the quotation above implies, musical training in a music therapy training course does not primarily serve an artistic or aesthetic purpose, but to enable the student to use music (or sounds) to get into a (therapeutic) relationships with another person. While the former aims at achieving beauty and perfection in the first place, the latter aims at finding an authentic way of expressing one's own thoughts and feeling by means of music. Therefore, musical training with a huge variety of instruments (including voice and body), and in particular musical training in free improvisation is at the centre of many curricula. As stated in some of the chapters above, it can be quite challenging – especially for (professional) musicians with a classical background – **to** refrain from focussing on aesthetic and technical aspects of making music, and instead to rely completely on intuition and expression. Thus, studying music therapy means to scrutinise one's own understanding of music, and to open up for new aesthetic experiences. These processes are of course closely connected to identity formation which leads us directly to the next topic.

6. Experiential learning, music therapy self-experience

Experiential learning is an umbrella term for the acquisition of knowledge through direct experience, including 'learning through reflection on doing' (cf. Wikipedia entry on "experiential learning"). According to Murphy (2014), experiential methods in music therapy are defined "as those in which the student is an active participant taking on the role of the client or the therapist and may include demonstrations, laboratory exercises, experiential exercises, group models, and/or personal therapy" (p. 18). Self-experience in the context of a therapeutic formation usually refers to the experience of a therapeutic process (individual or group setting) in the role of a client or patient. Bruscia (2014, p. 10) lists the following aims of self-experiences in the pedagogy of music therapy:

1. to impart knowledge and skill about how to practice music therapy;
2. to develop an understanding of how different methods of music therapy are experienced by clients;
3. to develop a capacity for deep empathy for clients; and
4. to develop self-awareness as a music therapist.

The significant role of self-experience in music therapy education is documented by the fact that the Austrian Music Therapy Act explicitly requires 200 hours (units) of self-experience as a mandatory prerequisite to be registered in the official Music Therapists List run by the Ministry of Health, i.e. to receive permission to work as a music therapist in Austria. According to the EMTR criteria, also a minimum of 200 hours of documented self-experience is required.

All music therapy training courses selected for this publication require some form of experiential learning and/or self-experience as part of the curriculum. In some courses, self-experience is integrated in the training course, some programmes require, or strongly recommend, self-experience at the student's own expense. The extent of experiential learning/self-experience ranges from one semester of experiential learning in group setting to three years of continuous self-experience in individual and group setting (90 hours resp. 180 hours, i.e. 270 hours in total). Again, these huge differences between the training programmes are partly because of different foci in the practical work, and partly because of different philosophies and traditions of education. Finally, due to financial reasons, individual self-experience is not affordable for all students, and therefore it is not a mandatory part of the curriculum in many cases. We argue that economic reasons should not be the decisive factor for the exclusion of an indispensable part of therapeutic formation. In particular, if students – for example, when starting a Bachelor's programme immediately after finishing high-school – are lacking life experience, it seems crucial to allow personal growth and identity formation with the help of 'as if therapy' processes that encourage and support self-inquiry, reflection, and personal insight. Fortunately, the need to pursue a debate about the status of self-experience and self-development within healthcare therapy trainings has been realized, and it seems both necessary and warranting to further discuss these issues with respect to music therapy training programmes (e.g. Edwards, 2013).

7. Evaluation procedures concerning quality of teaching

The environment and the structures of the European higher education system have changed dramatically during the last two decades. Not only because of the Bologna Process, but also because of the demographic change and geopolitical developments making education to one the most important resources in Europe. While some complain about the excessive bureaucracy, others praise the opportunities of facilitated international exchange (e.g. Erasmus). However, accreditation of training programmes, quality assurance, assessments, quality audits, and evaluations are, meanwhile, part of the vocabulary of every music therapist who belongs to the staff of an academic training programme. Thus, it is not surprising that evaluation procedures concerning the quality of teaching are a regular feature in all of the ten music therapy training programmes. In our opinion, – apart from the mandatory evaluation processes – in music therapy training courses, it seems to be warranting to cultivate a practice of giving and receiving feedback between teachers and students which might also serve as a role model for the therapists-to-be.

8. PhD programmes in music therapy

To date, there is only a limited number of PhD programmes in music therapy in Europe. One of the first programmes – and through its international orientation the most prestigious in Europe – is the PhD programme at Aalborg University in Denmark, which was established in 1993. A PhD programme at the Augsburg University, Germany, has been in existence since 2008. The two youngest PhD programmes started in 2013 at the University of Music and Performing Arts Vienna, Austria, and at LUCA, School of Arts, campus Lemmens, KULeuven, Belgium, respectively. The growing number of PhD students in music therapy documents the academic development of music therapy leading to mounting scientific evidence of music therapy. This seems crucial, as music therapy – as an academic profession – still has to struggle with the demarcation with respect to the esoteric use of music as a means of "healing" or "well-being". PhD programmes in music therapy are also important for the reputation in academic contexts, and concerning the endeavours for legal recognition of music therapy. One of the prominent tasks for the future of academic developments in Europe is professional networking of PhD students. A first step in this direction has been taken with an international pre-conference seminar on PhD research in music therapy that will take place at the European Music Therapy Conference 2016 in Vienna, Austria.

Outlook

The aim of this book was to provide both an up-to-date overview of all European music therapy training courses and a more detailed description of selected training programmes focussing on core contents of music therapy education, such as musical training, internships, and self-experience. Thus, this publication may serve as a complementary contribution in trying to document the status of European music therapy. In 2015, the first issue of Approaches was dedicated to music therapy in Europe, co-edited by Hanne Mette Ridder and Giorgos Tsiris. In their editorial of this special issue, Ridder and Tsiris stress the importance of 'thinking globally, acting locally', stating: "At the same time, we attempt to explore a number of overarching themes and questions pertaining to training, supervision, regulation and theory that resonate with various music therapy communities globally and seem to shape the ways that music therapy is defined" (p. 7). We, as co-editors of this book, tried to take up the thread and to further elaborate the debate regarding music therapy education and training. And, again borrowing from Ridder and Tsiris "any attempt to document professional development, thus, is not a matter of simply collecting facts; it is an interpretative process" (p. 7). "Theme and variations" – the title and the motto of this book – can be seen as the "score". In the first instance it is only black ink on white paper – no more, no less. But it only comes to life, i.e. a score becomes sound, when there are people who engage in an interpretative and transformative process. This is our aspiration for and with this book: we hope that music therapists in Europe and beyond will use these pages to pursue the debate about the pivotal question: what does it take to become a good music therapist? The answer cannot be found in this book – but maybe it serves for asking good questions and for composing new variations...

References

Bruscia, K.E. (2014). Introduction. In K.E. Bruscia (Ed.), *Self-experiences in music therapy education, training, and supervision* (pp. 9-17). Gilsum: Barcelona.

Edwards, J. (2013). Examining the role and functions of selfdevelopment in healthcare therapy trainings: A review of the literature with a modest proposal for the use of learning agreements. *European Journal of Psychotherapy & Counselling, 15* (3), 214-232. DOI: 10.1080/13642537.2013.811278

Murphy, K.M. (2014). Ethical considerations in experiential learning. In K.E. Bruscia (Ed.), *Self-experiences in music therapy education, training, and supervision* (pp. 18-26). Gilsum: Barcelona.

Reissenberger, K. (1970). *Versuch einer Überschau musiktherapeutischer Bemühungen innerhalb des europäischen Raumes* [Attempt of an overview of music therapeutic efforts within the European area]. Unpublished diploma thesis, Akademie für Musik und darstellende Kunst Wien, Vienna.

Ridder. H.M., & Tsiris, G. (2015). 'Thinking globally, acting locally': Music therapy in Europe. *Approaches: Music Therapy & Special Music Education, Special Issue 7*(1), 3-9.

Timmermann, T., Schmidt, H.U., Fitzthum, E., & Stegemann, T. (2013). Notwendigkeit von vergleichbaren Basisstrukturen und Basisinhalten musiktherapeutischer Ausbildungen – ein Modellentwurf [The necessity of camparable basic structures and core contents of music therapy training courses – a proposal] *Jahrbuch der Musiktherapie* (Vol. 9, pp. 71-84). Wiesbaden: Reichert.

Internet link to the Austrian Music Therapy Act:

https://www.ris.bka.gv.at/GeltendeFassung.wxe?Abfrage=Bundesnormen&Gesetzesnummer=20005868)

14   Contributors

Bonde, Lars Ole, PhD

Lars Ole Bonde. PhD. Professor in music therapy at Aalborg University (DK). Professor of music and health at the Norwegian Academy of music (N). Publications on music therapy, music psychology, music education and music theatre. Music therapist (DMTF), certified clinical supervisor. Music producer. Associate editor of Nordic Journal of Music Therapy. Current research projects: Music and public health, Music therapy for people suffering from schizophrenia, Monograph on the Danish Composer Bent Lorentzen. Numerous publications on theory and practice of music therapy, music psychology, music education, music theatre. (For an overview of publications and projects, see www.vbn.aau.dk)

contact: lobo@hum.aau.dk

De Backer, Jos, Prof. Dr.

Professor and coordinator Music Therapy at the Leuven University College LUCA, School of Arts, campus Lemmens. Senior researcher at LUCA, School of Arts and KULeuven. Head of the Music Therapy Department at the University Psychiatric Centre K U Leuven, campus Kortenberg. Boardmember Consortium Research and Education 8 universities. Past President of the European Music Therapy Confederation (EMTC).

contact: jos.debacker@luca-arts.be

Fitzthum, Elena, Dr. sc. mus.

Music therapist, psychotherapist and supervisor with over 30 years of experience in a variety of clinical settings. Elena Fitzhum is chair of the Viennese Institute of Music Therapy (WIM) and co-editor of WIM's book series Viennese Contributions to Music Therapy. She is also a lecturer at the University of Music and Performing Arts Vienna and at the Zurich University of the Arts. Her theoretical work is focussed on the history and development of music therapy.

contact: fitzthum@aon.at

Konieczna-Nowak, Ludwika, Dr.

Dr Ludwika Konieczna-Nowak – head of music therapy programme at The Karol Szymanowski Academy of Music in Katowice, in her clinical work focused on adolescents with emotional and behavioral challenges. Vice president of the Polish Music Therapists' Association. Editor-in-chief of the Polish Journal of Music Therapy. She holds MA in music theory from The Karol Szymanowski Academy of Music in Katowice with postgraduate diploma in music therapy from The Karol Lipiński Academy of Music in Wrocław and PhD from The Fryderyk Chopin University of Music in Warsaw. She continued her education at the School of Music, University of Louisville (Kentucky, USA).

She is active as clinician, educator and researcher, presenting and publishing internationally. Her recent interest includes aesthetic aspects of music therapy and music therapy as a support for developing resilience in youth at risk.

contact: muzykoterapia@am.katowice.pl

Lecourt, Edith

Edith Lecourt is Full professor emeriti at the University Sorbonne Paris City/Paris Descartes. Recently retired she still has the responsibility of five doctorates in the arts therapies (3 in plastics arts therapies + 2 in music therapy).

She is clinical psychologist, musician (clarinetist), psychoanalyst (specialized in group analysis), music therapist. She developed an articulation between group analysis and music therapy during the eighties. The application is the practice of a Group Analytic Music Therapy, based on a reflection on the place of sound (and music) in the development of human being, through relationship (the musical interval is a metaphor of this relation).

She was (with Jost and Guilhot) at the beginning of the professional development of music therapy in France during the seventies, through a co-foundation of the first association (1969), and of the first training (beginning of the seventies), and of the French Revue of Music Therapy (1980-2015).

She created the first Masters of Arts therapies and the Doctorate. She created a specialization on group analysis for psychologists (Master degree). She wrote many books and chapters (some translated in Italian, Spanish, Chinese, English, Polish, Greek, German), and a lot of articles.

She is principally president of the French Federation of Group Analysis, and vice-president of the French Association of Music Therapy (which she has co-founded with Pennec and Verdeau Pailles in 1980).

contact: edith.lecourt@orange.fr

Lindahl Jacobsen, Stine, PhD

Stine Lindahl Jacobsen is Associate Professor and Head of MA Programme of Music Therapy at Aalborg University in Denmark. Her main lecturing areas since 2008 include music therapy improvisation skills, group music therapy skills and music therapy assessment. Yearly since 2011 she lectures at University of Applied Sciences Würzburg-Schweinfurt in Germany and also lectures in Austria, Spain and Norway. She has published various articles and chapters in the area of working with children and families at risk and in the research area of standardized music therapy assessment tools and effect studies. As part of her PhD in 2012 Jacobsen developed the music therapy tool "Assessment of Parent-Child Interaction"

(APCI). Currently she trains and certifies music therapists from around the world, who work or have an interest in working with families.

contact: slj@hum.aau.dk

Mercadal-Brotons, Melissa, PhD, MT-BC, SMTAE

Director of the Music Therapy Master Program and Coordinator of Research and Master Programs at the Escola Superior de Música de Catalunya (ESMUC). She is also a professor in the department of Pedagogy and coordinates the research group "Música i Creació Musical", recognized as emerging group by the AGAUR (Agency for the management of University and Research grants of the Generalitat de Catalunya).

As a music therapist, she is involved in various music therapy clinical programs and research projects, especially in the area of geriatrics and dementia. She has published extensively both nationally and internationally. She is a co-author, along with her music therapist colleague Patrícia Martí, of the books "Music therapy Manual in Geriatrics and Dementia: Theory and Practice" (2008), "Manual of Music Therapy in Medicine" (2010) and "Music, Music Therapy, and disability "(2012) published by the JIMMS publisher.

Currently, she is the Chair of the Publications Commission of the World Federation of Music Therapy (WFMT) and the Spanish Delegate of the European Music Therapy Confederation (EMTC).

contact: melissa.mercadal@esmuc.cat

Paipare, Mirdza, MA

Mirdza Paipare is a graduate of the Vitola Latvian Music academy in Riga. She holds an MA in Music and Health care and has completed studies in Music Therapy, doctoral studies in musicology and joint Supervisor training programme of Riga Stradina University and Belfast Royal University.

She is currently docent and director of the Music Therapy programme at Liepaja University and Riga Stradins University, President of the Latvian Association of Music Therapy and formerly a representative at the European Music Therapy Confederation (2006-2013). Her research interests include music education, music therapy, and peak experiences in music.

contact: mirdza.paipare@liepu.lv

Roth, Katie, BA (Ed) (Hons)

Katie Roth holds a BA in Primary Education and Music from the University of Exeter, UK. She has lived in Latvia for seventeen years, working as an English teacher, special needs classroom assistant, and most recently as a trainee music therapist. She will graduate from the Liepaja University Music Therapy MA programme in July 2016. Her clinical focus is on children with emotional, social and behavioural difficulties in mainstream schools and orphanages. Her reseach interests include developing mixed methods approaches to investigating music therapy process.

contact: keitijaroth@gmail.com

Schmid, Johanna, MMag. art.

Johanna Schmid has completed a degree in Music Therapy at the University of Music and Performing Arts Vienna and holds a diploma in Musicology from the University of Vienna. She lives in Vienna and Upper Austria. At the moment she works as a music therapist in the field of acute psychiatry, psychiatric day care for adults, children- and adolescents psychosomatics but also with people with intellectual and multiple handicaps. Her special clinical interest lies in the field of Music Trauma Therapy and Transcultural Psychiatry. In spring 2017, she will finish an additional qualification in Music Trauma Therapy at the Freies Musikzentrum München. She enjoys spending her spare time as a musician and songwriter of the indie-folk band "Fräulein Hona", who will release their second album in autumn 2016.

contact: hannaschmid@gmx.at

Schmidt, Hans Ulrich, Prof. Dr.

Study of music pedagogics (Hamburg), music therapy (Hamburg, Vienna), medicine (Hamburg). Doctor for psychosomatic medicine at Hamburg University Hospital. Director of MA programme and Research Centre for Music and Health, Leopold Mozart-Centre, University of Augsburg. Private therapeutical practice in Hamburg. Member of scientific committee of dmtg. Publishing: Books, articles.

contact: hansulrichschmidt@phil.uni-augsburg.de

website: www.hu-schmidt-psychotherapie.de

Stegemann, Thomas, Univ.-Prof. Dr. med. Dr. sc. mus.

Thomas Stegemann studied guitar (Los Angeles, USA), medicine, and music therapy. He is a child and adolescent psychiatrist, a licensed music therapist, and a family therapist. Since 2011 he serves as Professor of Music Therapy and Head of the Department of Music Therapy at the University of Music and Performing Arts in Vienna, Austria. Main research areas: Music therapy and neurobiology, receptive music therapy with children and adolescents, music therapy with families

contact: stegemann@mdw.ac.at

website: www.thomasstegemann.at

Suvini, Ferdinando M., Dr. MA MT

Ferdinando M. Suvini, born in Milan, graduated in cello and studied composition has worked with leading organizations (Teatro alla Scala) and has played all over the Europe. Professor at the Conservatory of Music in Milan, Cagliari and Sassari. Holds Music Therapy Master in UWE University of the West of England, Bristol. Clinical activities with ASD children and in Oncological Hospital. Teacher of Music Therapy in Conservatorio of Ferrara (MA), Conservatorio of L' Aquila and in the main Private Training Courses in Italy (Milan, Bologna, Florence, Assisi). President of the Italian Association for Professionals of Music Therapy (AIM) since 2002. Vice President of European Confederation of Music Therapy (EMTC) since 2004. Member of the Scientific Commission in two World Congresses (Oxford and Buenos Aires) and in three European Conference (Eindhoven, Cadiz and Oslo). Speaker at international conferences. Publishes books and articles in specialized journals; Italian Site Manager of the Time A-Reserach Project on Music Therapy in ASD in 2016 start the doctoral programme (PhD) in Music Therapy at the Aalborg University (Denmark).

contact: ferdinando.suvini@conservatorioferrara.it

Timmermann, Tonius, Prof. Dr.

Study of paedagogy in Münster (1969 – 1975), music therapy in Vienna (1978 – 1981). Trainings in breath therapy and systemic constellations. Clinical practice: psychiatry, psychotherapy and psychosomatics (1981 – 1987). Research and graduation (Dr.rer.biol.hum.) at the University of Ulm, Department for Psychotherapy (1987 – 1990). Professor at the University of Augsburg. Head of the Master training in Music Therapy and the Research Center for Music and Health (2003 – 2015). Private therapeutical practice in Munich. Publishing: books, articles and music.

Homepage: www.timmermann-domain.de

Van Wuytswinkel, Luk, Prof.

Master music education, specialisation in music theory - scripture (fugue).

Professor in Music (Luca, campus Lemmens), coordinator harmony with a major in music therapy and music education and music therapy counselor BA.

contact: luk.vanwuytswinkel@luca-arts.be

Watson, Tessa, Convenor, MA Music Therapy (University of Roehampton)

Tessa Watson is a music therapist and trainer with over 20 years experience in various clinical settings. Currently Convenor of the MA Music Therapy at the University of Roehampton, Tessa also has a clinical post in an NHS community team for people with learning disabilities. She is one of the Editors of the British Journal of Music Therapy and holds several roles within the British Association for Music Therapy.

contact: Tessa.watson@roehampton.ac.uk

15 Appendix – Table of European music therapy training programmes

Country	Institution/ Training course	Bachelor	Master	Diploma	other [4]	costs [5] (EUR)	duration (semesters)	private	state-run
Albania	-	-	-	-	-	-	-	-	-
Andorra	-	-	-	-	-	-	-	-	-
Austria	Universität für Musik und darstellende Kunst (see chapter 3)	-	-	x	-	none (ÖH fee: 18.7)	8	-	x
	Universitäts-Lehrgang Musiktherapie – Kunstuniversität Graz	-	-	-	x	~13,080 (in total)	8	x	-
	University of Applied Sciences Krems	x	x	-	-	363,00	6/4	-	x
Belarus	-	-	-	-	-	-	-	-	-
Belgium	LUCA, Campus Lemmens (see chapter 4)	x	x	-	-	~860,00 (per year)	6/4	-	x
	Artevelde Hogeschool	x	-	-	-	340,00 (per year)	4	?	?
	Aream asbl	-	-	-	x	2,500 (per year)	4	x	-
Bosnia and Herzegovina	-	-	-	-	-	-	-	-	-
Bulgaria	BAMT	-	-	x	-	?	8	x	-
Croatia	University of Zagreb	-	-	-	x	800,00 (per year)	4	x	-
Cyprus	-	-	-	-	-	-	-	-	-
Czech Republic	Charles University	-	-	-	x	6,500 (per year)	?	-	x

Country	Institution/ Training course	Bachelor	Master	Diploma	other[4]	costs[5] (EUR)	duration (semesters)	private	state-run
Czech Republic	Technical University Liberec	-	-	-	x	?	?	-	x
	University Plzeň	-	-	-	x	?	2	-	x
	University Palacký	-	-	-	x	538.7 (in total)	3	-	x
	Akademie Tabor	-	-	-	x	1,016 (in total)	6	x	-
	Akademie alternativa	-	-	-	x	346.7	6	x	
Denmark	Aalborg University (see chapter 5)	x	x	-	x	none	6/4/6	-	x
Estonia	Tallinn University	x	x	-	-	840 (per year)	6	-	x
	Estonian Academy of Music and Theatre	-	-	-	x	1800 (in total)	6	-	x
Finland	Karelia University of Applied Sciences[6]	x	-	-	-	?	7	?	?
	University of Jyväskylä	-	x	-	-	92.3 (per year)	4	-	x
	Eino Roiha Institute	-	-	-	x	4,500 (per year)	6	x	-
France	Atelier de Musicotherapié de Bourgogne	-	-	-	x	4,407[7]/ 2,034[8] (in total)	4	x	-
	Atelier de Musicotherapié de Bourdeaux	-	-	-	x	1,650[9]/ 840[10] (in total)	2	x	-
	Université Paul Valéry Montpellier III	-	-	x[11]	-	7,000+ 3,500[12]/ 3,150+ 1,500[13]	4/2	-	x

Country	Institution/ Training course	Bachelor	Master	Diploma	other[4]	costs[5] (EUR)	duration (semesters)	private	state-run
France	Université de Nantes	-	-	x	-	7,320 (in total)	6	-	x
	Université Paris-Descartes (see chapter 6)	-	x	-	-	12,667[14] (in total)/ ~300[15] (per year)	4	-	x
	C.I.M. Centre International de Musicothérapie	-	-	-	x	7,250 (in total)	4	x	-
Germany	SRH Hochschule Heidelberg	x	x	-	-	520 BA 530 MA (per month)	7/4	x	-
	Universität Augsburg (see chapter 7)	-	x	-	-	500	6	-	x
	Universität der Künste Berlin	-	x	-	-	330 (per month)	6	-	x
	Hochschule für Musik und Theater Hamburg	-	x	-	-	285.5	6	-	x
	Hochschule Magdeburg-Stendal	-	x	-	-	500	4	-	x
	Theologische Hochschule Möckern-Friedensau	-	x	-	-	1,781	6	x[16]	-
	Westfälische Wilhelms-Universität Münster	-	x	-	-	218.6	4	-	x
	Hochschule für angewandte Wissenschaften Würzburg-Schweinfurt	-	x	-	-	1,500	4	-	x
	Musiktherapeutische Arbeitsstätte Berlin	-	-	-	x	12,750 (in total)	8,5	x	-
	Institut für Musiktherapie Berlin	-	-	x	-	205 (per month)	6	x	-
	Institut für Gestalttherapie u. Gestaltpädagogik Berlin	-	-	-	x	270 (per month)	9	x	-

Country	Institution/ Training course	Bachelor	Master	Diploma	other[4]	costs[5] (EUR)	duration (semesters)	private	state-run
Germany	Institut für imaginative Psychotherapie und Musik – GIM Buchholz	-	-	-	x	4,715[17]	8 +	x	-
	Akademie für angewandte Musiktherapie Crossen	-	-	-	x	6,275 (in total)	6	x	-
	Europäische Akademie für Psychosoziale Gesundheit (FPI) Hückeswagen	-	-	-	x	11,375 [18] (in total)	8	x	-
	Freies Musikzentrum München	-	-	-	x	16,780 [19] (in total)	7	x	-
	Deutsche Akademie für Entwicklungs-Rehabilitation e.V. München	-	-	-	x	7,625 (in total)	6	x	-
	Zukunftswerkstatt therapie kreativ, Neukirchen – Vluyn	-	-	-	x	8,544 – 8,739 (in total)[20]	4	x	-
	Europäische Akademie der Heilenden Künste	-	-	-	x	7,650 (in total)	4	x	-
	Hamburger Institut für gestaltorientierte Weiterbildung	-	-	-	x	~7,460 (in total)	8	x	-
Greece	Aristotle University Thessaloniki	x[21]	-	-	-	?	10	-	x
	Music Therapy Center	-	-	-	x	?	?	x	-
Hungary	ELTE/Eötvös University Budapest	-	-	-	x	482.3	4	-	x
	Liszt Academy of Music Pécs	-	-	-	x[22]	?	4	x	-
Iceland	-	-	-	-	-	-	-	-	-
Ireland	Irish World Academy of Music and Dance	-	x	-	-	9,720[23]/ 19,478[24] (in total)	4	?	?

Country	Institution/ Training course	Bachelor	Master	Diploma	other[4]	costs[5] (EUR)	duration (semesters)	private	state-run
Italy	Associazione APE – Genova	-	-	x	-	?	6	x	x
	Associazione APIM Genova-Torino	-	-	x	-	1,500	6	x	x
	Associazione Artem Udine	-	-	x	-	?	6	x	x
	Associazione "G. Ferrari" Padova	-	-	x	-	?	6	x	x
	Associazione ISFOM – Napoli	-	-	x	-	?	6	x	x
	Associazione La Linea dell' Arco – Lecco	-	-	x	-	?	6	x	x
	Associazione Music Space Bologna	-	-	x	-	?	6	-	x
	Associazione Stratos – Bari	-	-	x	-	?	6	x	x
	Centro Musica e Arte – Firenze	-	-	x	-	6,600 (total)	4	-	x
	Centro Studi e Ricerche Milano	-	-	x	-	?	6	x	x
	Centro Studi Alto Vicentino Thiene	-	-	x	-	?	6	x	x
	CEP – Assisi	-	-	x	-	1,200	4	x	x
	Cooperativa Oltre – Roma	-	-	x	-	?	6	x	x
	Cesfor Bolzano	-	-	x	-	1,500	6	x	x
	Conservatorio "A. Casella" L' Aquila	-	-	x	-	600	4	-	x
	Conservatorio "F. Dall' Abaco" Verona	-	-	x	-	1,200	4	-	x

Country	Institution/ Training course	Bachelor	Master	Diploma	other[4]	costs[5] (EUR)	duration (semesters)	private	state-run
Italy	Conservatorio Statale di Musica "Luisa D'Annunzio" Pescara	x	-	-	-	2,400 (total)	6	-	x
	Conservatorio "G. Frescobaldi" Ferrara (see chapter 8)	-	x	-	-	1,000	4	-	x
	Conservatorio non Statale "P. Mascagni", Università Pisa, Livorno	-	-	-	x	2,600	4	-	x
Latvia	Liepaja University (see chapter 9)	-	x	-	-	1,410 (per year)	6	-	x
	Riga Stradiņš University	-	x	-	-	~1,800 (per year)	5	-	x
Liechtenstein	-		-	-	-	-	-	-	-
Lithuania	Vilnius Pedagogical University / Lithuanian University of Educational Sciences	-	x[25]	-	-	112.8 (per subject, 6 ECTS)[26]	3	-	x
Luxembourg	-		-	-	-	-	-	-	-
Malta	-		-	-	-	-	-	-	-
Moldavia	-		-	-	-	-	-	-	-
Monaco	-		-	-	-	-	-	-	-
Montenegro	-		-	-	-	-	-	-	-
Netherlands	ArtEZ Conservatorium Enschede	x	-	-	-	1,906 (per year)	8	-	x
	Zuyd University of Applied Sciences [27]	x	x	-	-	1,835 (per year)	8/4	-	x

Country	Institution/ Training course	Bachelor	Master	Diploma	other [4]	costs [5] (EUR)	duration (semesters)	private	state-run
Nether-lands	Hogeschool van Arnhem en Nijmegen	x	-	-	-	1,906 (per year)	8	-	x
	HU – University of Utrecht	x	-	-	-	1,906 (per year)	8	-	x
	Hogeschool Stenden	x	-	-	-	1,951 (per year)	8	-	x
Norway	Norwegian Academy of Music	x	x	-	-	no fees	6/4	-	x
	University of Bergen	-	x	-	-	no fees	10	-	x
Poland	Maria Curie-Skłodowska University	-	-	-	x	1,500 (in total)	3	-	x
	Akademia Muzyczna w Krakowie	-	-	-	x	?	5	-	x
	Karol Lipiński Academy of Music	x	x	-	-	no fees	6/4	-	x
	The Karol Szymanowski Academy of Music (see chapter 10)	x	x	-	x	no fees/ no fees/ 1,600 (in total)	6/4/4	-	x
	Grażyna and Kiejstut Bacewicz Music Academy	x	-	-	-	?	6	-	x
	Akademia Pomorska	-	-	-	x	359.8	3	?	?
Portugal	Universidade Lusíada de Lisboa	-	x	-	-	?	4	x	-
	Instituto Politecnico do Porto – Escola Superior de Educaçao	-	-	-	x	?	3	-	x
Republic of Mace-donia	-		-	-	-	-	-	-	-

Country	Institution/ Training course	Bachelor	Master	Diploma	other [4]	costs [5] (EUR)	duration (semesters)	private	state-run
Romania	-	-	-	-	-	-	-	-	-
Russia[28]	-	-	-	-	-	-	-	-	-
San Marino	-	-	-	-	-	-	-	-	-
Serbia	Association of Music Therapists of Serbia/Hatorum	-	-	-	x	960 (per year)	8	x	-
Slovakia	?	?	?	?	?	?	?	?	?
Slovenia	University of Ljubljana	-	x[29]	-	-	?	4	-	x
Spain	Universidad Autonoma de Madrid	-	x	-	-	5,800 (in total)	3	-	x
	Universidad de Barcelona Les Heures	-	x	-	-	6,040 (in total)	4	-	x
	ESMUC Barcelona (see chapter 11)	-	x	-	-	5,750 (in total)	4	-	x
	Universidad de Cádiz	-	x-	-	x[30]	4,400 (Master programme)	4/3	-	x
	Universidad Nacional de Educación a Distancia	-	-	-	x	340	1	-	x
	Centro de Investigación Musicoterapeutica (CIM)	-	x	-	-	2,600 (in total)	4	x	-
	Universidad Pontificia De Salamanca	-	x	-	x[31]	2,700/ 1,080	4/2	x	-
	Universitat Ramon Llull/ Universitat Pompeu Fabra	-	x	-	-	6,900 (in total)	4	x	-

Country	Institution/ Training course	Bachelor	Master	Diploma	other [4]	costs [5] (EUR)	duration (semesters)	private	state-run
Spain	Universidad de Zaragoza	-	-	-	x	2,100 (in total)	4	-	x
	Istituto Música, Arte y Proceso	-	x	-	x[32]	2,225 (per year)/ 6,230 (in total)	6/2	x	-
	Musitando	-	-	-	x	2,500 (per year)	6	x	-
	Universidad Católica de Valencia	-	x-	-	-	3,100 (in total)	2	x	-
	Universitat de Vic	-	x	-	-	?	4	x[33]	x
	Centro Benenzon Espana	-	x	-	-	1,450 (in to-tal/ levels)	?	x	-
	Casa Baubo/Escuela International de Música, y Musicoterapia	-	x	-	-	6,000 (in to-tal)	8	x	-
Sweden	Musikhögskolan Ingesund	x	-	-	-	no fees	3	-	x
	Royal College of Music Stockholm	-	x	-	x	no fees[34] /7,200[35]	4/?	-	x
	Expressive Arts – Stockholm	-	-	-	x	~1,351	2/6[36]	x	-
Switzer-land	Zürcher Hochschule der Künste Zürich[37]	-	x	-	x	~3,800 (a,b), ~5,741 (c)	8 (a) /10-12 (b) / ~8 (c)	-	x
	Ecole Romande de Musi-cothérapie	-	-	-	x	17,704 (in total)	6	x	-

Country	Institution/ Training course	Bachelor	Master	Diploma	other [4]	costs [5] (EUR)	duration (semesters)	private	state-run
Switzerland	Forum Musikth. Weiterbildung Schweiz	-	-	-	x	21,677 (in total)	8	x	-
	Integrative Musiktherapie SEAG	-	-	-	x	?	?	x	-
	Orpheus Schule für Musiktherapie	-	-	-	x	22,855 (in total)	8	x	-
Turkey	-		-	-	-	-	-	-	-
Ukraine	-		-	-	-	-	-	-	-
United Kingdom	University of the West of England	-	x-	-	-	7,111 (per year)	6	-	x
	Anglia Ruskin University	-	x	-	-	10,377[38]/ 12,208[39] (in total)	4	-	x
	Nordoff-Robbins Music Therapy UK[40]	-	x	-	-	9,492[41]/ 16,612[42] (in total)	4	x	-
	Guildhall School of Music and Drama	-	x	-	-	17,407[43]/ 39,573[44]	4	-	x
	Roehampton University (see chapter 12)	-	x	-	-	16,566[45]/ 22,037[46] (in total)	4 (full-time) 8 (part-time)	-	x
	Queen Margaret University	-	x	-	-	6,789[47]/ 14,324[48]	4	-	x
	University of South Wales	-	x	-	-	6,626	6	-	x

Notes:

4   for example further training, advanced training, post graduate training,...
5   per semester, if not specifically mentioned
6   as of 1999, course closed now
7   if the candidate is employed somewhere (continuous education)
8   if the candidate is not employed (basic/initial training)
9   if the candidate is employed somewhere (continuous education)
10   if the candidate is not employed (basic/initial training)
11   "Diplôme Universitaire de Musicothérapie (1er niveau)" (four semesters) and "Diplôme Universitaire de Musicothérapie (2ème niveau)" (two semesters)
12   if the candidate is employed somewhere (continous education), 1er niveau and 2ème niveau
13   if the candidate is not employed, 1er niveau and 2ème niveau (basic/initial training)
14   if the candidate is employed somewhere (continous education)
15   if the candidate is not employed (basic/initial training)
16   not private as such, but church-operated
17   excluding fees for training therapy and supervision
18   including training therapy and examination costs
19   including training therapy and examination costs
20   depending on the price of the eclective subjects, not including costs for self-therapy and supervision
21   Musicology study with specialisation on Music Therapy, Bachelor's program which is recognized as a Master's level program since it is 5 years
22   not an explicit Music Therapy, but an Art Therapy course, specialisation in either Music, Dance-Movement or Art Therapy
23   for EU-students
24   for Non-EU-students
25   Art Therapy specialization (30 credit points) integrated in the Social Work Master's programmes at the Social Communication Institute
26   there's the possibility to study for free
27   two different courses: fulltime Bachelors' four-year course and a two-year Master course
28   at the moment there is no training course yet established (according to H.-H. Decker-Voigt)
29   in Art Therapy (drama, dance-movement, music, fine arts)
30   postgraduate diploma in music therapy (60 ECTS)
31   "Experto en Musicoterapia" (= expert in Music Therapy)
32   postgraduate course in Guided Imagery and Music
33   Universitat de Vic is a publicly owned and privately run foundation (Universitat de Vic)
34   EU-Students
35   Non-EU-Students
36   one-year training in "Short Music Travel" (KMR) and a further two-year (altogether three-year) Music Therapy training in the Bonny Method of Guided Imagery and Music (BMGIM)
37   the ZHdK offers three courses: a) Master of Advanced Studies (MAS) in Clinical Music Therapy, b) psychotherapeutic on-the-job-training, c) Upgrade Master of Advanced Studies (MAS) for professionally trained music therapists
38   for UK/EU-students
39   for international students
40   offers two training courses with the same conditions, one in London, one in Manchester
41   for UK/EU-students, personal therapy is not included in these costs
42   for international students, personal therapy is not included in these costs
43   for UK/EU-students
44   for international students
45   full-time
46   part-time
47   for UK/EU-students
48   for international students

References

Aasgaard, T., & Trondalen, G. (2004, July). Music therapy in Norway. *Voices Resources.* Retrieved March 18, 2014, from http://testvoices.uib.no/community/?q=country/monthnorway_july2004

Abrams, B. (2013). Guided Imagery and Music, Bonny method. In K. Kirkland (Ed.), *International Dictionary of Music Therapy* (pp. 54-55). London: Routledge.

Bonde, I.. (2007, January). Music therapy in Denmark. *Voices: A World Forum for Music Therapy.* Retrieved April 16th, 2014, from http://testvoices.uib.no/?q=monthdenmark_january2007

Bonde, L. & Pedersen, I. N. & Wigram, T. (2002). *A comprehensive guide to music therapy.* London: Jessica Kingsley Publishers

Colwell, C. (2013). Orff Music therapy. In K. Kirkland (Ed.), *International Dictionary of Music Therapy* (pp.95). London: Routledge.

Damen, O. (2004). Wesenszüge anthroposophischer Musiktherapie [Characteristics of anthroposophic music therapy]. In G. Beilharz (Ed.), *Musik in Pädagogik und Therapie* (pp.265-283). Stuttgart: Verlag Freies Geistesleben.

De Backer, J. & Coomans, A. (2006, February). Music therapy in Belgium. *Voices Resources.* Retrieved March 18, 2014, from http://testvoices.uib.no/community/?q=country-of-the-month/2006-music-therapy-belgium

De Backer, J. (2013). Psychoanalytical music therapy. In K. Kirkland (Ed.), *International Dictionary of Music Therapy* (pp.104). London: Routledge.

Erkkilä, J. (2002, May). Music therapy in Finland. *Voices: A World Forum for Music Therapy.* Retrieved March 18, 2014, from http://testvoices.uib.no/?q=country-of-the-month/2002-music-therapy-finland

Erkkilä, J. (2008, March). The state of music therapy in Finland. *Voices: A World Forum for Music Therapy.* Retrieved March 18, 2014, from http://testvoices.uib.no/?q=country-of-the-month/2008-state-music-therapy-finland

Ferrone, A. M. (2004, June). Music therapy in Italy. *Voices: A World Forum for Music Therapy.* Retrieved March 17, 2014, from http://testvoices.uib.no/?q=country/monthitaly_june2004

Florschütz, T. M. (2009). Anthroposophische Musiktherapie [Anthroposophic Music Therapy]. In H.-H. Decker-Voigt & E. Weymann (Eds.), *Lexikon Musiktherapie* (pp. 33-41). Göttingen: Hogrefe Verlag.

Frohne-Hagemann, I. (2009). Integrative Musiktherapie [Integrative Music Therapy]. In H.-H. Decker-Voigt & E. Weymann (Eds.), *Lexikon Musiktherapie* (pp. 214-219). Göttingen: Hogrefe Verlag.

Forgács, E. (2008). Music therapy in Hungary. *Voices: A World Forum for Music Therapy.* Retrieved March 17, 2014, from http://testvoices.uib.no/?q=country/monthhungary_ september 2008

Gustorff, D. (2009). Nordoff/Robbins-Musiktherapie (Schöpferische Musiktherapie) [Nordoff/Robbins music therapy/Creative Music Therapy]. In H.-H. Decker-Voigt & E. Weymann (Eds.), *Lexikon Musiktherapie* (pp. 353-356). Göttingen: Hogrefe Verlag.

Gustorff, D. (2001). Schöpferische Musiktherapie (nach Nordoff/Robbins) [Creative Music Therapy (after Nordoff/Robbins)]. In H.-H. Decker-Voigt (Ed.), *Schulen der Musiktherapie* (pp. 208-241). München: Ernst Reinhardt Verlag.

Güvenc, R. O. (2006, March). Music therapy in Turkey. *Voices: A World Forum for Music Therapy, Resources.* Retrieved March 17, 2014, from http://testvoices.uib.no/ community/?q=country/monthturkey_march2006

Kirkland, K. (2013). Benenzon model of music therapy. In K. Kirkland (Ed.), *International Dictionary of Music Therapy* (pp.13). London: Routledge.

Metzner, S. (2001). Psychoanalytische Musiktherapie [Psychoanalytical music therapy]. In H.-H. Decker-Voigt (Ed.), *Schulen der Musiktherapie* (pp. 33-54). München: Ernst Reinhardt Verlag.

Lindahl Jacobsen, S. (2012). Denmark. *Imagine Magazine, 3 (1)*, p. 76-77. Retrieved from http://imagine.musictherapy.biz/Imagine/color_of_us.html

Paipare, M. (2013). Integrative-eclectic music therapy. In K. Kirkland (Ed.), *International Dictionary of Music Therapy* (pp.64-65). London: Routledge.

Paulander, A.-S. (Ed.)(2008, May). Music therapy in Sweden. Voices Resources. Retrieved March 17, 2014, from http://testvoices.uib.no/community/?q=country/monthsweden_ june2008

Psiliteli, M., Vaiouli, P. (2013, June). Response to music therapy in Greece [Letter to the editor]. Voices: A World Forum for Music Therapy.

Quin, A. (2005, April). Music therapy in Romania. *Voices Resources.* Retrieved March 17, 2014, from http://testvoices.uib.no/community/?q=country/monthromania_ may2005

Sabbatella, P.L. (2004, March). Music therapy in Spain. *Voices Resources.* Retrieved March 17, 2014, from http://testvoices.uib.no/community/?q=country/monthspain_ march2004

Smeijsters, H. (2009). Methoden der psychotherapeutischen Musiktherapie [Methods of psychotherapeutic music therapy]. In H.-H. Decker-Voigt & E. Weymann (Eds.), *Lexikon Musiktherapie* (pp. 267-273). Göttingen: Hogrefe Verlag.

Smeijsters, H. & Vink, A. (2010, September). Developments in music therapy in the Netherlands. *Voices Resources.* Retrieved March 17, 2014, from http://testvoices.uib. no/community/?q=country/monthnetherlands_october2010

Stachyra, K. (2013, April). In search of the golden mean – our way to music therapy. *Voices Resources*. Retrieved March 17, 2014, from http://testvoices.uib.no/com munity/?q=fortnightly-columns/2013-search-golden-mean-our-way-music-therapy

Tsiris, G. (2013). Nordoff-Robbins music therapy. In K. Kirkland (Ed.), *International Dictionary of Music Therapy* (pp. 93). London: Routledge.

Tsiris, G. (2011, May). Music therapy in Greece. *Voices Resources*. Retrieved March 17, 2014, from http://testvoices.uib.no/community/?q=country-of-the-month/2011-music-therapy-greece

Voigt, M. (2001). Musiktherapie nach Gertrud Orff – eine entwicklungsorientierte Musik-therapie [Music therapy after Gertrud Orff – a development-oriented music therapy model]. In H.-H. Decker-Voigt (Ed.), *Schulen der Musiktherapie* (pp. 242-262). München: Ernst Reinhardt Verlag.

Watts, E. (2004, February). Music therapy in Bosnia-Herzegovina: an introduction. *Voices Resources*. Retrieved March 19, 2014, from http://testvoices.uib.no/com munity/?q=country-of-the-month/2004-music-therapy-bosnia-herzegovina-intro duction

Zanchi, B. & Suvini F. & Ferrara, C. & Bodrato, B. & Borghesi, M. & D'Ulisse E. & Ca-sotti, A. (2005, November). Perspective of music therapy in Italy: past, present and future. A search for a national identity. In *Music Therapy Today*, Vol. VI, Issue 4, pp.1686-1695.

Internet sources

AUSTRIA:

www.oebm.org, Österreichischer Berufsverband der MusiktherapeutInnen

http://www.mdw.ac.at/mbm/mth/, Universität für Musik und darstellende Kunst (Wien)

http://www.fh-krems.ac.at, University of Applied Sciences (Krems)

http://www.impg.at/gramuth/, Universitätslehrgang Musiktherapie – KUG (Graz)

BELGIUM:

http://www.lemmensinstituut.be, Lemmensinstitut (Leuven)

http://associatie.kuleuven.be/ , LUCA Faculty of the Arts (Leuven)

http://www.arteveldehogeschool.be/creatieve-therapie, Arteveldehogeschool (Ghant)

http://www.aream.be, Aream asbl (Brussels)

https://voices.no/community/?q=country-of-the-month/2006-music-therapy-belgium, Voices, Country of the month Belgium

BULGARIA:

http://bulgarianmusictherapy.com, BAMT (Sofia)

CROATIA:

http://www.erf.unizg.hr Faculty of Education and Rehabilitaion Sciences (Zagreb)

CZECH REPUBLIC:

http://www.icv.upol.cz Institut celoživothního vzděkávání (Olomouc)

http://www.pedf.cuni.cz/?lang=en, Faculty of Education, Charles University (Prague)

http://www.tul.cz/en/, Faculty of Education, Technical University (Liberec)

http://www.zcu.cz, University of Plzeň (Plzeň)

http://akademiealternativa.cz, Akademie alternativa (Olomouc)

http://www.akademietabor.cz/studium, Akademie Tabor (Prague)

DENMARK:

http://www.en.aau.dk, Aalborg University (Aalborg)

http://www.mt-phd.aau.dk, Aalborg University, PhD programme (Aalborg)

ESTONIA:

http://www.musictherapyworld.net/WFMT/Regional_Information_files/Fact%20Page_
Estonia%20(2013).pdf, WFMT/ Music Therapy Today: Fact Page Estonia

www.tlu.ee Tallinn University (Tallinn)

FINLAND:

https://www.jyu.fi/hum/laitokset/musiikki/en/studies/mmt/therapy, University of Jyväskylä (Jyväskylä)

http://www.karelia.fi/, Karelia University of Applied Science (Outokumpuu/Joensuu)

http://www.ers.fi, Eino Roiha Säätiö

http://www.wfmt.info/Musictherapyworld/modules/wfmt/w_docs10.htm, WFMT Sym-
posium 1999, Scandinavian Music Therapy Education

FRANCE:

http://www.musicotherapie-federationfrancaise.com, Federation Francaise du Musicothérapie

http://ateliers-ambx.net, Atelier Musicothérapie de Bordeaux (Parempuyre)

http://www.amb-musicotherapie.com, Atelier de Musicothérapie de Bourgogne (Dijon)

www.musicotherapie-montpellier.fr, Université de Paul Valéry Montpellier III (Montpellier) http://www.musicotherapie-nantes.com, Université de Nantes (Nantes)

http://www.scfc.parisdescartes.fr, Université Paris Descartes (Paris)

http://www.musicotherapie.info, C.I.M. (Paris, Aix en Provence)

GERMANY:

http://www.musiktherapie.de, Deutsche musiktherapeutische Gesellschaft (DMtG)

http://www.higw.de, Hamburger Institut für gestaltorientierte Weiterbildung (Hamburg)

http://www.hochschule-heidelberg.de/de/studium/masterstudium/musiktherapie/, SRH Hochschule Heidelberg (Heidelberg)

http://www.philso.uni-augsburg.de/lmz/institute/mmm/Musiktherapie/, Universität Augsburg (Augsburg)

http://www.udk-berlin.de/sites/musiktherapie/content/index_ger.html, Universität der Künste (Berlin)

http://www.hfmt-hamburg.de, Hochschule für Musik und Theater Hamburg (Hamburg)

https://www.hs-magdeburg.de/studium/weiterbildung/methoden-musiktherapeutischer-forschung-und-praxis.html, Hochschule Magdeburg-Stendal (Magdeburg-Stendal)

http://www.thh-friedensau.de/christliches-sozialwesen/master-of-arts-musiktherapie/, Theologische Hochschule Friedensau (Möckern-Friedensau)

http://www.uni-muenster.de/Musiktherapie/, Westfälische Wilhelms-Universität (Münster)

http://mmt.fhws.de, Hochschule für angewandte Wissenschaften Würzburg-Schweinfurt

http://www.musiktherapeutische-arbeitsstaette.de, Musiktherapeutische Arbeitsstätte (Berlin)

http://www.musiktherapieberlin.de, Institut für Musiktherapie (Berlin)

http://www.iggberlin.de/weiterbild-gmusik.htm, Institut für Gestalttherapie und Gestaltpädagogik (IGG) (Berlin)

http://www.gim-therapie.de, Institut für imaginative Psychotherapie und Musik GIM (Buchholz)

http://www.musiktherapie-crossen.de, Akademie für angewandte Musiktherapie (Crossen)

http://www.freies-musikzentrum.de/index.html?/Aktuell_Semester/fortbildungen/musiktherapie.html, Freies Musikzentrum München

http://akademie-muenchen.de/2014/, Deutsche Akademie für Entwicklungs-Rehabilitation e.V. München

http://www.eag-fpi.com/integrative_musiktherapie.html, Europäische Akademie für Psychosoziale Gesundheit (FPI) (Hückeswagen) http://www.zukunftswerkstatt-tk.de, Zukunftswerkstatt (Neukirchen-Vluyn)

http://www.eaha.org, European Academy of Healing Arts (Klein Jasedow)

GREECE:

http://www.musictherapy-center.gr, Music Therapy Center of Thessaloniki (Thessaloniki)

HUNGARY:

http://www.art.pte.hu, University of Pécs (Pécs)

http://www.elte.hu/de, ELTE/ Eötvös University Budapest (Budapest)

IRELAND:

http://www.ul.ie/graduateschool/course/music-therapy-ma, University of Limerick

http://www.irishworldacademy.ie/postraduate-programmes/ma-music-therapy/faq/, Irish World Academy of Music and Dance (Limerick)

ITALY:

http://www.consaq.it, Conservatorio Statale di Musica Alfredo Casella (L'Aquila)

http://www.formazioneamps.it, Associazione Musicoterapeuti Professionisti Siciliani

http://www.apollon-musicoterapia.it, Apollon Istituto di Musicoterapia (Cosenza)

http://www.musicoterapiaumanistica.it, A.I.M.U., Associazione Italiana Musicoterapia Umanistica (Napoli)

http://musicaterapia.it, Associazione Professionale Italiana Musicoterapisti (Genova, Torino, Lecco)

http://www.musicoterapia.fvg.it Associazione Regionale Musicoterapia del Friuli Venezia Giulia "Il Flauto Magico" (Udine)

www.cesfor.bz.it, Cesfor – Centro studio e formazione (Bolzano)

http://www.conservatorioverona.it, Conservatorio di Verona Everisto Felice dall' Abaco (Verona)

https://www.facebook.com/pages/ISFOM-Istituto-Formazione-Musicoterapia/246551648722517, Istituto Formazione Musicoterapia (ISFOM) (Napoli)

www.musicoterapiadinamica.net Scuola di Musicaterapia Dinamica (Firenze)

http://www.artiterapielecce.it Istituto di Artiterapie e Scienze Creative (Lecce)

http://www.musicspaceitaly.it, MusicSpace Italy (Bologna)

http://www.cittadelladiassisi.it/musicoterapia/, Scuola di Musicoterapia di Assisi (Assisi)

http://www.artiterapie.it, Centro Artiterapie di Lecco (Lecco) http://scuoladimusicoterapiaumanistica.wordpress.com, Scuola di Musicoterapia Umanistica Giulia Cremaschi Trovesi (Padova)

http://www.cooplda.it, La Linea dell' Arco (Lecco)

http://www.associazionestratos.it, Stratos (Bari)

http://www.musicoterapiaveneto.it, F.I.M. / Musicoterapia Veneto (Padova)

http://www.associazioneprogettoespressione.it, APE (Associazione Progetto Espressione) (Genova)

http://www.conspe.it, Conservatorio Luisa D'Annunzio (Pescara)

LATVIA:

http://www.liepu.lv, Liepaja University (Liepaja)

http://www.rsu.lv, Riga Stradiņš University (Riga)

LITHUANIA:

http://www.muzikosterapija.lt, Lietuvos muzikos terapijos asociacija (Vilnius)

LUXEMBOURG:

http://www.sana-via.lu, Sana Via Institut (Schwebach)

MALTA:

http://catsmalta.org, C.A.T.S.Malta

NETHERLANDS:

http://www.artez.nl/conservatorium/Muziektherapie, ArtEZ Conservatorium (Enschede)

http://kenvak.hszuyd.nl, KenVaK Master of Arts Therapies (Heerlen)

http://www.zuyd.nl/studeren/studieoverzicht/creatieve-therapie, Zuyd Hogeschool (Heerlen)

http://www.han.nl/opleidingen/bachelor/de/kreatieve-therapie-de/vt/, Hogeschool van Arnhem en Nijmegen (Nijmegen)

https://stenden.com, Hogeschool Stenden (Stenden/Leuwaarden)

NORWAY:

http://www.uib.no, University of Bergen (Bergen)

http://www.nmh.no Norwegian Academy of Music (Oslo)

POLAND:

http://www.instytutmuzyki.apsl.edu.pl Akademia Pomorska (Slupsk)

www.am.katowice.pl, The Karol Szymanowski Academy of Music (Katowice) http://www.umcs.lublin.pl, Maria Curie-Skłodowska University (Lublin)

http://www.amuz.wroc.pl, Karol Lipinski Academy of Music (Wroclaw)

http://www.amuz.lodz.pl, Grażyna and Kiejstut Bacewicz Music Academy (Łódź)

PORTUGAL:

http://www.lis.ulusiada.pt, Universidade Lusíada de Lisboa (Lissabon)

http://musicoterapiaenportugal.blogia.com, Blog "Musicoterapia en Portugal"

SERBIA

http://www.muzikoterapija.rs/en/, The Association of Music Therapists in Serbia

SLOVAKIA:

www.arte-terapia.sk, Artea (Bratislava)

SLOVENIA:

https://www.pef.uni-lj.si, University of Ljubljana (Ljubljana)

SPAIN:

http://www.ub.edu, Universitat de Barcelona Les Heures (Barcelona)

https://www.ucv.es, Universidad Católica de Valencia (Valencia)

http://www2.uca.es, Universidad de Cádiz (Cádiz)

http://www.mastermusicoterapiauam.com, Universidad Autonoma de Madrid (Madrid)

http://www.isep.es, Universitat de Vic (Barcelona)

http://unizar.es/, Universidad de Zaragoza (Zaragoza)

http://www.centrobenenzonmusicoterapia.com, Centro Benenzon Espana (Valencia)

http://www.upsa.es, Universidad Pontificia de Salamanca (Salamanca)

http://www.agruparte.com, Istituto Música, Arte y Proceso (Vitoria-Gasteiz)

http://www.musitando.org, Musitando (Madrid)

http://www.uned.es/pfp-introduccion-musicoterapia/, Universidad National de Educación a Distancia

http://casabaubo-escuela.blogspot.com.es, Casa Baubo (Santiago de Compostela)

SWEDEN:

http://www.kau.se/musikhogskolan-ingesund, Musikhögskolan Ingesund (Arvika)

http://www.kmh.se, Royal College of Music (Stockholm)

http://www.expressivearts.se, Expressive Arts (Stockholm)

http://www.fmt-metoden.se, Functionally Oriented Music Therapy (FMT) (Uppsala)

SWITZERLAND:

http://www.musictherapy.ch, Schweizerischer Fachverband für Musiktherapie, Association Professionelle Suisse de Musicothérapie

http://www.zhdk.ch/index.php?id=9864, Zürcher Hochschule der Künste (Zürich)

http://www.erm-musicotherapie.ch Ecole Romande de Musicothérapie (Genève)

http://www.orpheus-schule.org, Orpheus Schule für Musiktherapie (Schafisheim)

http://www.fmws.ch, Forum musiktherapeutischer Weiterbildung Schweiz (Schwaderloch)

http://www.eag-fpi.com/integrative_musiktherapie.html, Integrative Musiktherapie SEAG (Rorschach)

TURKEY:

http://tumata.com, Traditional Turkish Music Research and Promotion Society (Istanbul)

UNITED KINGDOM:

http://www.bamt.org, British Association for Music Therapy

http://www.nordoff-robbins.org.uk, Nordoff Robbins Music Therapy (London)

http://www.gsmd.ac.uk, Guildhall School of Music and Drama (London)

http://www.roehampton.ac.uk, University of Roehampton (London)

http://www.qmu.ac.uk, Queen Margaret University (Edinburgh)

http://www.uwe.ac.uk, University of the West of England (Bristol)

http://courses.southwales.ac.uk/courses/1233-ma-music-therapy, University of South Wales (Newport)

http://www.lesliebunt.com, Leslie Bunt, Music therapist

GENERAL:

http://www.ecarte.info, European Consortium for Arts Therapies Education (ECArTE)

http://imagine.musictherapy.biz, Imagine Magazine. Early childhood Music Therapy

http://www.musictherapyworld.net, World Federation of Music Therapy (WFMT)

http://www.aamta.org, Association for Anthroposophic Medicine & Therapies in America

http://ami-bonnymethod.org, Association for Music and Imagery

http://www.ehea.info, European Higher Eduacation Area

http://www.eua.be, European University Association

http://www.auswaertiges-amt.de, Auswärtiges Amt (Germany)

forum zeitpunkt · zeitpunkt musik

Music Therapy and Psychodrama
The benefits of integrating
the two methods
By Heidi Fausch-Pfister
8°. 152 p, 14 b/w-ill., pb
(978-3-89500-899-3)

"That which is raised up from the ocean of the subconscious by music therapy can be pulled ashore with the help of psychodramatic elements." This effect is illustrated with striking examples from child and adolescent psychiatry, neurology and adults' therapy, which are analysed in a sophisticated way. Various psychodramatic techniques and instruments supplement the current methods of music therapy. The author explains in what ways psychodramatic instruments and techniques can reinforce the therapeutic process in music therapy. They are particularly helpful in intensifying and structuring the therapeutic process, focusing on a theme, applying what has been learned during therapy in daily life, and transferring problems of everyday life into the therapy. In putting these ideas into practice, the reader is aided by practical suggestions and methodological advice. The book provides a valuable and interesting read for students of music and art therapy, therapists, pedagogues, music teachers and keen amateurs.

forum zeitpunkt · zeitpunkt musik

Receptive Music Therapy
Theory and Practice
Ed. by Isabelle Frohne-Hagemann
8°. 332 p, 15 b/w-ill., pb
(978-3-89500-564-0)

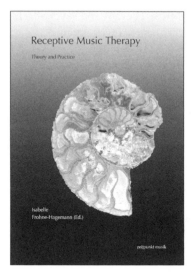

Although listening to music in music therapy has a much longer tradition than active music therapy, receptive music therapy in European countries has been strongly neglected for many years. The German edition of this book, published in 2004, is the first to present the most important methods of receptive music therapy in one volume. This volume presents the English edition. 18 well-known European authors present forms of receptive music therapy, which focus on both theoretical and practical aspects. The spectrum of methods and clinical applications is broad: receptive music therapy as or in psychotherapy (f. ex. Guided Imagery and Music, Regulative Music Therapy, Integrative Music Therapy), as Sound Guided Trance, In Depth Relaxation Therapy, in Anthroposophic Music Therapy, etc.. Various case studies of adolescent and adult patients illustrate how to work in different clinical contexts. Theoretical questions are discussed concerning topics such as music and (alterated states of) consciousness, music and emotion, music and imagery, music and developmental relationships and music and earliest childhood. This volume provides an extensive overview of Receptive Music Therapy in Germany, Denmark, Sweden and Luxembourg and will provide new impulses for those music therapists and psychotherapists who because of language problems have not been able to follow these European developments in Receptive Music Therapy.

forum zeitpunkt · zeitpunkt musik

Hearing – Feeling – Playing
Music and Movement
with Hard-of-Hearing and Deaf Children
By Shirley Salmon
8°. 288 p, 23 b/w-ill., 24 charts, pb.
(978-3-89500-621-0)

Music and dance for hard-of-hearing and deaf children is not yet offered as a matter of course or as an extra-curricular activity in European schools and has not been widely documented in German speaking countries. This volume focuses on presenting diverse approaches as well as the foundations for the use of music and movement. On the one hand, the importance of music and movement as developmental support or therapy is outlined and, on the other hand, the right to music and movement or dance for everyone is upheld. Within this context, approaches and principles from Germany and Austria as well as from Italy, England, Denmark and Canada are presented. "Hearing - Feeling - Playing" refers to acoustic, vibratory, tactile, emotional and social stimuli as well as to their perception and their active realization. The importance and the possibilities of music-making and listening for all is described in the forward by the world famous percussionist Evelyn Glennie, who, after developing a hearing disorder in her childhood, learned to use her whole body as a source of resonance. The book examines the fundamentals of each approach as well as the diverse educational and therapeutic goals and methods. At the same time vital issues in the education of people with hearing loss, in music and movement education, music therapy and inclusive education are addressed. This book aims to address, inform and inspire specialists from educational and therapeutic fields as well as parents and those with hearing loss. The central question in practical settings remains: which approach involving music and/or movement, which methods and which form of participation - be it in education, remedial help and support or therapy - can be of benefit to the children in question?

forum zeitpunkt · zeitpunkt musik

Lively Children's Choir
joyful – playful – dancing.
Incentives and Examples
By Christiane Wieblitz
8°. 312 p, 131 b/w-ill.,
133 printed music items, pb.,
(978-3-89500-772-9)

A practical handbook for working vocally with children aged 8 to 12 years. Singing means the development of the personality... and this involves more than just performing songs. Illustrated with vivid photographs, drawings and examples in musical notation and clearly organized according to topics this book contains:

Breathing, speech and vocal games
Rhythmic and movement games
Games for listening and invention
Dances and songs
Aids to acquiring a sense of pitch and intonation
Models for the structuring of a lesson
Detailed background information and explanation of all games and topics

From the Foreword by Regina Pauls:
The interconnection between singing, making music, speaking and movement is made transparent and is presented in a practical way through the musical competence of the author. She has been able to give a pictorial description of the children's involvement with their artistic activities. Many varied forms of teaching and learning, methods, means, and the experience of aesthetic processes are introduced, which enable the reader to understand pleasurably the learning process from experience to structure.